CW00502434

P U B W A

IN

North & West Cumbria
Cumberland

Alan Shepley

COUNTRYSIDE BOOKS
NEWBURY, BERKSHIRE

First published 1996
© Alan Shepley 1996

All rights reserved. No reproduction
permitted without the prior permission
of the publisher:

COUNTRYSIDE BOOKS
3 Catherine Road
Newbury, Berkshire

ISBN 1 85306 397 5

Designed by Mon Mohan
Cover illustration by Colin Doggett
Photographs and maps by the author

Produced through MRM Associates Ltd., Reading
Printed by Woolnough Bookbinding Ltd., Irthlingborough

Contents

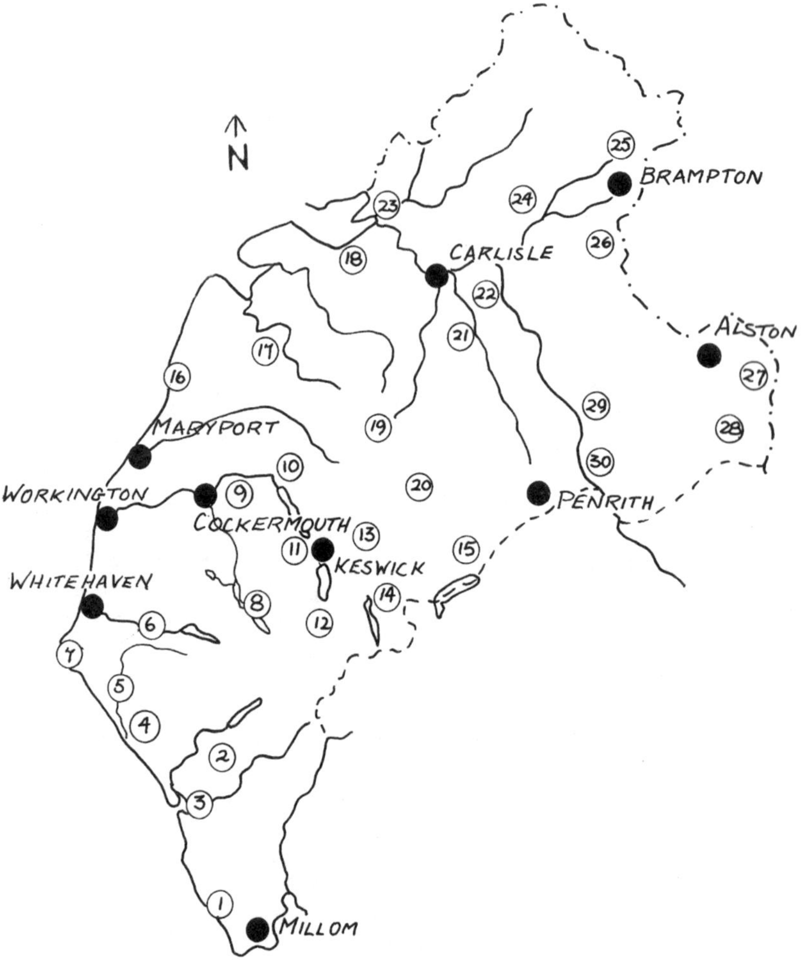

Area map showing the locations of the walks

Introduction

This collection of walks covers the part of Cumbria which used, for 800 years, to be called Cumberland (a companion volume, *Pub Walks in South Cumbria*, covers those areas which were Westmorland, the Furness district of Lancashire and a corner of North Yorkshire). Slightly over half the county, it is still a big area and stretches from Millom, in the south-west, to beyond Bewcastle, in the north-east, and from St Bees, on the west coast, to Nenthead in the east. In such an extensive territory it is not surprising that there is a wide variety of countryside to explore.

Three large sections are designated in special ways. Rather over half of the Lake District National Park is included, with the highest point in England (Scafell Pike) and the northern and western lakes themselves within its boundaries. The Solway Coast is an Area of Outstanding Natural Beauty and about a quarter of the North Pennines AONB runs along most of the eastern boundary (including Cross Fell, the highest point of the Pennines). In landscape terms the county divides up into the west coast, the Lakes, the Solway Coast, the Solway Plain, the Border country, the Eden valley and the Pennines. Walks are set in each of these areas. In addition, of course, there are some sites which are of national and international conservation interest, like St Bees Head, a multitude of venues where history has been made over and over again, and some extremely interesting museums. There will, surely, be a choice to please most moods and most occasions.

As a matter of policy this book has been compiled in accordance with the guidelines for the writers of path guides produced by the Outdoor Writers' Guild and each walk has been re-visited during its preparation. Do, however, remember that the countryside is a workplace as well as somewhere to enjoy yourself and that consequent changes (most of which may be perfectly legal) are surprisingly frequent. Walk descriptions are, perforce, like a snapshot in time and the details can only be as accurate as it was practicable to make them at that moment. It is wise to carry the Ordnance Survey Landranger 1:50 000 map with you as a means of checking the route when you find yourself in doubt – each walk includes a reference to the appropriate sheet number. I always find that passing the time of day with the local people you meet along the way, especially the farmers, is not only informative about the exact route but also provides a wealth of local and up-to-date information, which no book can ever do. Very rarely indeed is such a chat anything but unalloyed pleasure.

Most walks are along relatively easy routes. Distance is indicated, but time will depend on the weather and the composition of the party. Where there is a clear danger, e.g. because of cliffs, this is mentioned. As persistently sunny summers turn up only once every 300 years or so, the presumption must be that rain and mist are highly likely, especially near the mountains, and you should be prepared with the right clothing and footwear. Remember that cold, wet conditions can, and do, kill just as well as the more obvious dangers of snow and ice. Cumbrian soil gets as muddy as any in the country and routes which are bridleways, or go through gateways and farmyards where cattle churn up the ground, are likely to need boots (or, perhaps, wellingtons) more than most. Also, only you can know your own dog's likely behaviour in the countryside, but it is wise to assume that farm animals and dogs don't mix and, of course, it's the dog that is the visitor. Always remember to follow the Country Code.

Licensees and landlords of pubs have their own views, of course, on opening hours, eating your own food, on children and dogs, and on leaving your car in their car parks. The majority seem to me most affable and a pleasant word before you take the plunge will not go amiss. If in doubt, make use of the telephone to check opening and food times, especially on Sundays and during the winter months, particularly away from the main tourist venues. It is only possible to give an indication of the drinks and menus available and, in any case, many pubs now offer specials boards which are changed daily.

A good few of the pubs can be reached by public transport when they are on, or near to, a main road or close to a railway station and some of you will prefer this to car travel. Timetables change too frequently, however, for useful details to be included. Within the National Park the information centres usually have an annual publication of public transport services available. Elsewhere you will need to contact bus and rail operators direct.

Each time I put together a new set of walks I am ever more acutely aware that I owe a great debt to the shared experience with fellow walkers and the published information gathered by a host of writers who have gone before me. I thank them all and pray that I have succeeded in creating a worthwhile addition to those many guides which help others enjoy our countryside. I am firmly of the opinion that, despite the dangers of 'loving it to death', on balance, those who have joined in the experience that our land can give – like no other in the world, I think – will learn how to care for its future and ensure that it has one through the generations to come.

Alan Shepley
Spring 1996

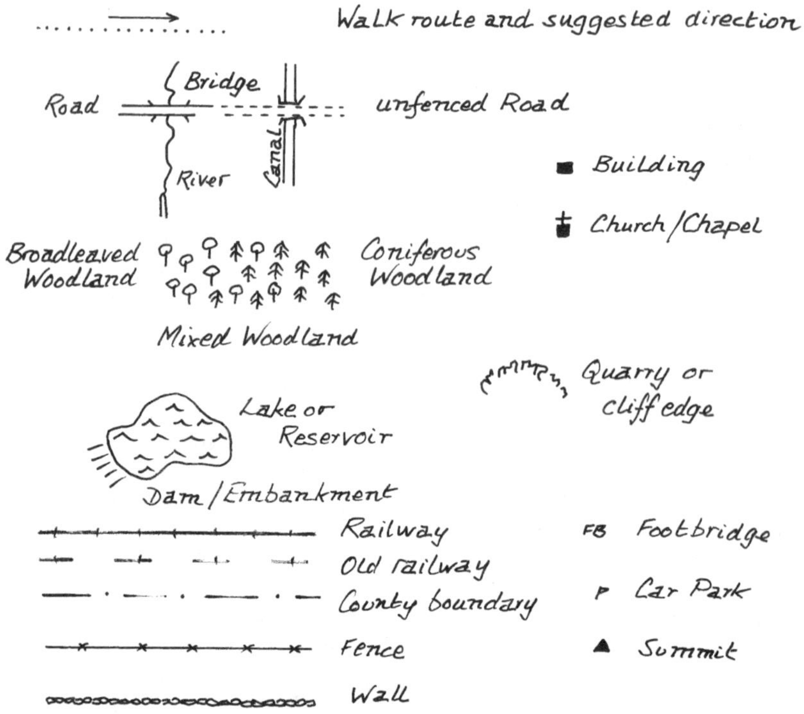

Key to sketch maps

Publisher's Note

We hope that you obtain considerable enjoyment from this book; great care has been taken in its preparation. However, changes of landlord and actual closures are sadly not uncommon. Likewise, although at the time of publication all routes followed public rights of way or permitted paths, diversion orders can be made and permissions withdrawn.

We cannot of course be held responsible for such diversion orders and any inaccuracies in the text which result from these or any other changes to the routes nor any damage which might result from walkers trespassing on private property. However, we are anxious that all details covering the walks and the pubs are kept up to date and would therefore welcome information from readers which would be relevant to future editions.

1 Kirksanton
The King William IV

Time has simply overtaken Kirksanton (the church of St Sancta, perhaps?) – its ecclesiastical centre has shifted to Whicham and the post office and shop are in Silecroft. The main road to the north out of Millom, which cuts it in two, is, itself, little more than a lane and the pub stands beside it at the top of the green on the corner of the turn towards the sea. Level crossings for the main west coast railway line trap the village between them. The pub building is well over 200 years old, the low beams of the stone-flagged bar are black with age and the fire in the range blazes brightly in winter. Old photographs of the locality decorate the walls.

The 'King Billy' is well known for its bar and restaurant food, which is served throughout the pub's opening hours. In the bar the selection offers all the standard fare as well as vegetarian alternatives. The restaurant menu is especially popular with local people for the beef stroganoff, amongst the variety of international tastes, all freshly prepared. But what better than to sit comfortably with home-made soup on a cold day, followed by entrecôte steaks in a Dijon mustard sauce with brandy and cream, and rounded off with a good cheese board? Children's portions are available.

This freehouse opens from 12 noon to 3 pm and 7 pm to 11 pm (10.30 pm on Sundays). The usual bitters are Jennings Cumberland and

Mitchell's Original plus a guest beer, and the mild is Whitbread. Guinness is the stout, Strongbow the cider and, unusually, the lager is Äyingerbrau. A select and interesting international wine list accompanies restaurant meals. Families are welcome throughout the pub and there is a public play area on the adjacent green for the children. Dogs are welcome in the bar. Overnight accommodation is also available.

Telephone: 01229 772009.

How to get there: Follow the A5093 from Millom or from the junction with the A595 just north of Silecroft.

Parking: A small amount of parking space is immediately outside the door and there is plenty more along the lane beside the green.

Length of the walk: 4½ miles. Map: OS Landranger 96 Barrow-in-Furness (pub GR 139807).

The far south-west of old Cumberland is a forgotten corner well worth exploring. Although the main road runs through the Whicham valley it is not of it and most traffic simply passes by. The mass of Black Combe dominates to the north and sweeps down to the sea at its foot. Man has been here for thousands of years and only in the last 200 has land transport come to prime importance, so you could imagine yourself, like your ancestors, coming over the estuary of the Duddon or direct from the sea.

The Walk

Turn right out of the pub door and walk around the green. Here Kirksanton's second church stood, until it sank in the boggy ground – the third was across the main road on the site of one of the modern bungalows. Turn to the right over the small beck and immediately cross the main road to the path marked for Pohouse. The track reaches the railway line in 30 yards and you need to cross through the gates with care. Follow the track to the right by the cottage and go up between the stoned banks cum hedges. It could well be rather wet underfoot as far as the swing left up the bank after the footbridge of old sleepers. Stay by the fence up to the rough stile. The view back already spans the dunes around Haverigg (with HM Prison and the wind farm in evidence) and north, along the coast, to Silecroft village and its caravan site by the surf-washed shore.

Keep to the right-hand wall and go up the old green track towards the buildings on the brow ahead. Pass through one gateway and bear to the right, through a second, just before the next cross-wall. Make your way up to the farm ruin and through the yard. In the fields to the right are several small stone circles, amongst which a Bronze Age urn has been found.

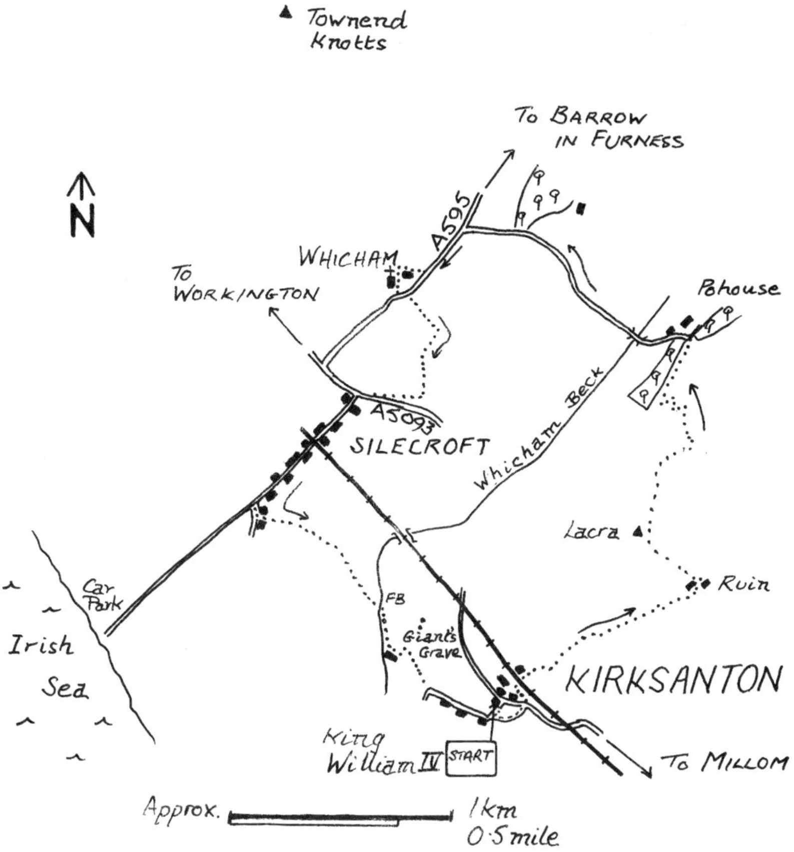

Close by was the site of the first Kirksanton church, perhaps as early as AD 350.

Leave the ruins by turning to the left along the track which goes over the brow of Lacra. Ahead is the whole wall of slates and shales which make up Black Combe. Townend Knotts is a little left, Pen End in front, and Cotley a little right. At 1,970 ft, it is not particularly high but, because it comes almost straight out of the sea, it towers above and catches the first of the cloud. Throughout the south Lakes it is said that if you can't see Black Combe it is raining and if you can it's going to! Follow the definite farm track and descend the face of the slope. Eventually reach zigzags and walk below the cliff and scree of Dog Crag down to the gate amongst the sycamores onto the lane opposite Pohouse.

Go to the left and drop a little to cross the beck and enter the National

Park. The lane climbs up amongst scatterings of gorse on rounded mounds of sandy soil, which were left when the glacier melted from the Whicham valley 10,000 years ago. On the right, below the wood, is Whicham Hall, where Robert the Bruce's Scots fought a skirmish with the local defenders during the great raid across the Solway and down the west coast in 1322.

At the main road junction go to the left for 300 yards, with great care for the traffic. This section of road is unavoidable and it is very narrow here, so be prepared for large HGVs followed by a line of cars. Take the second track to the right and walk along past the old school (now offering bed and breakfast) as far as the steps beyond. Turn left up these and enter the churchyard of St Mary's. This building was extensively altered in Victorian times but the south doorway is 12th century and still bears the marks made by archers sharpening their arrows on the soft red sandstone. The medieval font is of the same material. The bells in the cote on the west end are over 500 years old and are inscribed 'St Mary and St Michael pray for us'.

Leave the church by the same gate and walk to the main road. Go left for 50 yards and cross over to the footpath. Follow the left-hand boundary of the field and go straight ahead over the stile to the gate on the far side of the next field. Turn to the right through this, behind the water trough, and follow beside the right-hand boundary, past two more gates, to a stile in the corner. Bear to the right over this and take a second stile, onto the old road. Walk down and cross over the A5093, bearing left into Silecroft village, which seems to take its name from a medieval salt works. This is now the centre of a minor holiday trade and shows a pleasant face of old barns, house walls, and garden walls built of sea-rounded cobbles from the shore. Continue towards the sea, past the old buildings of the Miners Arms, and over the level crossing. Pass the old red telephone box on the right and Kellet House on the left and take the next lane to the left, signed for Southfield. (An addition is to walk another half mile to reach the National Park car park at the shingle shore.)

In 50 yards, a footpath bears off left, along a farmer's track, between two bungalows. Walk between the high, windblown hedges, which give shelter from the gales off the sea, to a stile into a field. Off to your left is the tip of an old mine and across the main road are the old maltings. Bear half-right and cross two more stiles to a footbridge to the left, where you meet the flood bank of the Whicham beck. Turn to the right on the far side and walk down towards the buildings of Standing Stones. Use the gate by the farm bridge and walk left through the yard. Follow the track as it bends left then right. At this second bend it is worth the minor diversion into the field, along another footpath, to look at the two standing stones called the Giant's Grave – of unknown age. Return to the track and go left to the lane and left again to return through Kirksanton to the pub.

2 Eskdale Green
The Bower House Inn

Eskdale Green, confusingly, doesn't have a green nor does it wholly lie in Eskdale, but straddles a low hause between that valley and Miterdale. The ancient Celtic name of Eskdale, 'the valley of the waters', might be applied with justice to most Lakeland valleys and it is the tumbling river Mite that flows fussily beneath the bridge beside the Bower House Inn, which is surrounded by gardens. The inn is certainly older than 1751 and was both a farm and an alehouse for many years. Today these characteristic Lakeland buildings are a top-rated hotel, conference centre, restaurant and old-world bar.

Great thought is given to the food here. An evening restaurant meal menu offers a wide choice; what about air-dried Cumberland ham with melon, followed by roast duckling in red wine and plum sauce, finished off with summer pudding? Guinea fowl, venison, and sea bass are specialities. If the lighter bar fare is your choice the range is still excellent – from ploughman's lunches to steak and kidney pie, from home-made soup to sandwiches and salads. Both vegetarian and children's menus are available. Bar food is served from 12 noon to 2 pm and 6.30 pm to 9.30 pm each day.

This is a freehouse. Bar hours are 11 am to 11 pm, except for Sundays, when they are 12 noon to 3 pm and 7 pm to 10.30 pm. The beers include Theakston Best Bitter and XB, Younger Scotch and Courage Directors. Guinness and Scrumpy Jack cider are on draught. The beer garden is delightful but there is no special provision for children. Dogs are welcome in the garden and free kennelling is provided for residents' pets. The restaurant is a non-smoking area.

Telephone: 019467 23244.

How to get there: The inn is just beyond the northern end of the village (and actually in the next parish of Holmrook). From the A595 turn at Gosforth and approach via Santon Bridge or take the lane just south of Holmrook. Alternatively, bear right for Gosforth at the foot of Eskdale.

Parking: There is a large car park to the rear, but please remember to ask at the bar if you wish to leave your car while you walk. A pleasant alternative is to use the Forest Enterprise car park and to make the inn the halfway point.

Length of the walk: 3 miles. Map: OS Landranger 89 West Cumbria (inn GR 131002).

This short and easy walk makes use of one of the many mature areas of forest which Forest Enterprise has opened up for general recreation in recent times and is in Miterdale, not Eskdale itself. A wide variety of trees are to be seen, birdlife is plentiful and the views up the valley are excellent.

The Walk

Turn right from the inn and follow the road towards Eskdale Green, passing the car repair shop and the village sign. Turn left up the next lane (there is no sign) and soon go past the school on your left. (An alternative, and interesting, approach to the whole walk is to arrive at this point by walking the half mile from the Eskdale Green station of the Ravenglass and Eskdale narrow gauge railway, past the entrance of the famous Outward Bound Centre.)

The lane continues past a large farm and the old mill beside the river Mite, then a bank barn dated 1905. At the bridleway sign, take a few steps out of your way to look at the old stone bridge amongst the trees. Return to the lane and continue ahead to the gate into Miterdale Forest. About a quarter of a mile further on, informal parking is provided and there is a picnic area beside the river.

Cross over the forest bridge and bear to the right along the track to the point at which a further track hairpins back to your left before the gate (there is no sign). The view up the valley to Great How is fine and buzzards, sparrowhawks and kestrels can often be seen against the sky.

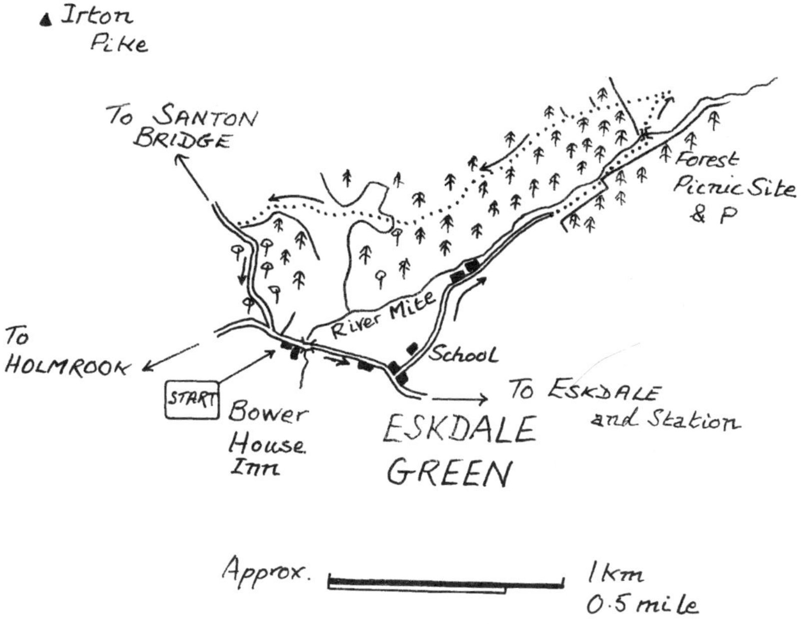

Walk on the bridleway below the wall back into the forest and enter the plantations of western hemlock and European larch with scattered old oak amongst them. Be prepared for muddy patches here after rain.

Pass a field on your right and cross over a well-made forest track at the beeches, taking just a few paces left before going right on more or less the same line as before. Continue beside the line of an old tumbledown wall amongst a mixture of trees and areas of rhododendrons. Go over a beck and past fine larches above the wall, with some Douglas fir on the left and the occasional sweet chestnut. Cross a ford diagonally and bear right through pines to a gate. Ignore the stone stile to the left and continue ahead, passing a small field to the left and reaching another on the right. At the gate on the left, bear half-right through the gap in the old bank and cross to the wall gap below the larch plantation. Follow the green track through bracken and across rocky fields. Muncaster Fell stands out to the left and Irton Pike dominates the view half-right, even though it is but 751 ft high.

At the gate, exit left onto the farm access track and walk along it, past a forest gate, to the road. Go down the hill and round the bend amongst coppices of hazel, sycamore and oak, looking out for traffic. At the Holmrook turn go left a few more yards to return to the inn.

3 Ravenglass
The Ratty Arms

The Ratty, in this case, is the 'La'al Ratty' (the narrow gauge Ravenglass and Eskdale Railway) which rattles its way up Eskdale to Boot from the separate station on the inland side of the main line from the pub. The Ratty Arms was created out of the old Furness Railway station for Ravenglass in 1974 and a conservatory area added on the platform side.

In the summer, food is served all day until 9.30 pm, and this is so for winter Saturdays too. Otherwise, the hours are 11 am (noon on Sundays) to 2.30 pm and 6 pm (7 pm on Sundays) to 9.30 pm. The menu is a wide and varied one, always offering pies, fish, chicken, hot and cold meats and pasta, with ploughman's lunches and salads, jacket potatoes and sandwiches for the slightly less hungry. There are special vegetarian and children's menus. The evening menu is supplemented with a range of starters, steaks and grills.

Beer drinkers will find a goodly choice at the bar. This is, again, open all day in the summer. Winter times are 11 am to 3 pm and 6 pm to 11 pm and all day Saturday (12 noon to 3 pm and 7 pm to 10.30 pm on Sundays). Beers include Jennings, Theakston, Ruddles and Webster's plus a guest beer, while the lagers are Carlsberg, Holsten and Labatt's and the stouts are Guinness and Murphy's. Both Scrumpy Jack and Strongbow ciders are served. A large patio area makes a pleasant beer garden. Well-behaved dogs are welcomed on a lead.

Telephone: 01229 717676.

How to get there: Turn at the sign for Ravenglass on the A595 and bear left to the pub after the second railway arch.

Parking: A small amount of parking is available on the old station approach. Immediately adjacent to the pub is a National Park car park.

Length of the walk: 4¾ miles, including visiting Muncaster Mill. Map: OS Landranger 96 Barrow-in-Furness (pub GR 085964).

The link up of the old port of Ravenglass, the Roman remains, Muncaster Castle and the Owl Centre, Muncaster Mill and the narrow gauge railway, plus the fell views, make this one of the outstanding venues for a walk in the whole of the North of England. It can, too, be combined with a trip up Eskdale or on the main West Coast line. The La'al Ratty has its own museum. There are no difficult climbs and the surfaces are reasonably dry under most conditions.

The Walk

Start from the main entrance of the pub by crossing diagonally left over the National Park car park and exit down the rear of Murrayfield Terrace. Turn left into the main village street at the side of the Pennington Arms. Fishing and pleasure boats are drawn up on the shore immediately opposite. It has been a port since pre-Roman times (they arrived as early as AD 79, calling it Glanoventa, then built their road over Hardknott, at the head of Eskdale – where there are the remains of a fort – to link the port with the settlement at Ambleside) with sheltered anchorage in the joint estuary of the Esk, the Mite and the Irt. Salmon, flounders and mussels are still fished for. The village is one of the locations used in Hugh Walpole's *Rogue Herries*, features at the start of W. G. Collingwood's *The Bondwomen* and is in numerous other minor prose and poetry works. You can walk along the shore but it is better to follow the street left past the cottages, many of which incorporate Roman stones – one house is dated 1689. The impressive Reading Room is much later at 1898.

Turn left along the top of the shore at the end of the street. If the tide is in, you will need to take the first track off to the left in 200 yards and then use the path along the top of the low clay cliff. Otherwise, stay on the shore as far as the ramp to the arch under the railway on the left. Shore birds call as you go and fishing stakes still straddle the estuary. Turn left again along a track to Walls House, dated 1885. It is worth the diversion of 50 yards to the left here to see Walls Castle, the remains of the Roman

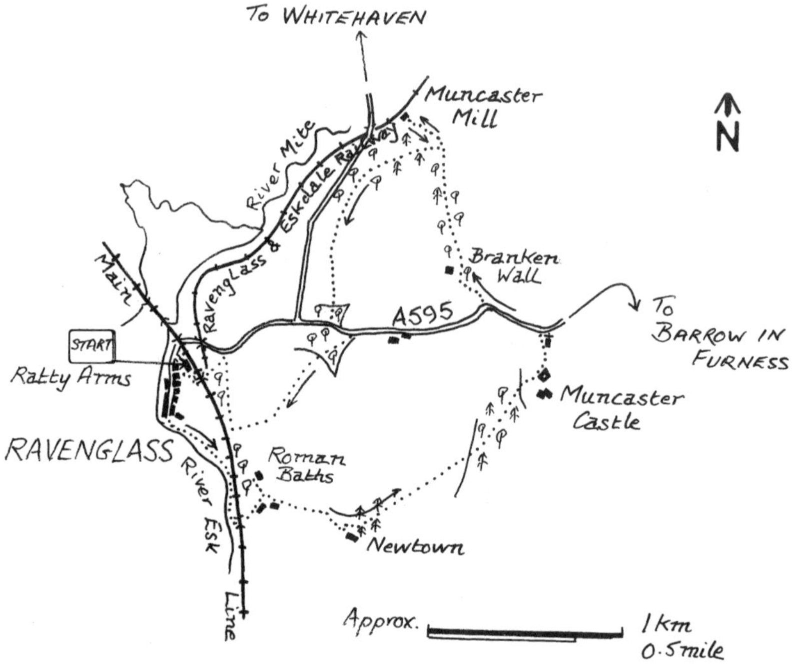

bath house and some of the highest standing Roman remains in the country. Return to Walls House and take the left fork, with the scent of resin from the pines and cedars in summer. Rise up gradually amongst rhododendrons and turn sharply left, underneath overhanging branches, 50 yards before the barn at Newtown. Go up again, through new oak plantings and then into spruce and pine. The view back from the field edge is across the estuary to the nature reserve on Drigg dunes and beyond to the Isle of Man.

Bear slightly to the left to pass by the remains of a gate and stile in the middle of the field and leave the rocky knoll to your right. Move slowly right amongst the thistles and into the low dip, where a yellow-topped post marks the path. Away to the right, across Eskdale, lies Corney Fell. A gate ahead in the high wall leads through the woods and gardens of Muncaster Castle, the route being marked by more yellow-topped posts. When you reach the cut lawns, head towards the arched gateway beyond the pond.

Here is the café and shop of the castle and directly across is the Owl Centre (which includes other birds too, and there are free-flying demonstrations on summer afternoons). The land was granted to the

Penningtons in 1208 and the castle is still lived in by them. The claim is that the 'Luck of Muncaster', a glass drinking bowl given to his host by the fleeing Henry VI after the battle of Hexham in 1464, protects their ownership so long as it remains unbroken. A defensive pele tower rests on Roman foundations and the building was extensively added to in the 1860s. The castle is open from March to October, except for Mondays, and the Owl Centre and gardens are open all year.

Return to the arch and walk between this and the high wall to the left, passing the entrance to the garden centre. About 100 yards further along, on the right, is the delightful small church of St Michael. Its origins may go back to the visit of Henry VI. Return to the driveway and walk up another 100 yards to the main A595. Go left up the hill on the footway beneath a row of large Corsican pines on the far side. At the bend, go straight ahead on the bridleway signed for Muncaster Mill. The fields on the left here are the site of a justly famous local show on August Bank Holiday Monday. Before you reach the buildings of Branken Wall farm a gate to the right sets you on a permissive path which swings round the farm, through the wood, and rejoins the footpath on the far side. Walk ahead along a shallow, dry valley to cross the ridge. At the far side the track forks. The right-hand branch gives an opportunity to drop down to the restored and working water mill, which produces stone ground flour (there is a La'al Ratty station here if you want an alternative return to the village or to go up Eskdale).

Return to the fork and go left to contour round the hill through woods. The path becomes a track and drops to a crossing (a permissive path to and from the mill may be open to the right). Turn to the left and rise a little amongst parkland trees and through fields to the crest. The river Mite is in view below and the Isle of Man out to sea. At the top the view behind is to Wasdale to the north. Walk down by the side of the wood to the road and cross over with care, turning left along the footway to the bend. Go right into the wood along the path by a small ghyll, with old oaks on the far side amongst some fine young sycamores. At the field, follow the clear path to a kissing-gate at the junction of fences and bear right on the far side to a stile by a gate at the bottom in a gap in the line of trees. Turn right on the far side along a track and pass the entrance to the caravan site. Go left on the footpath by the gateposts at the road.

Immediately before the footbridge over the main line railway there is a path to the right into the yard and station of the La'al Ratty. This opened in 1875 to transport iron ore from upper Eskdale to Ravenglass and the main line. Originally 3 ft gauge, it was converted to 15 inches in 1913 and ran until the granite quarries closed in 1953. Enthusiasts reopened it for tourist traffic in 1960 and it attracts many thousands each year. Steam trains run in all months of the year and there is a museum, workshops and a shop. Return to the Ratty Arms over the footbridge.

4 Gosforth
The Wheatsheaf Inn

Nowadays, Gosforth stands back from the main coast road but it remains the centre for shops and other facilities for Wasdale, Blengdale and the surrounding coastal farmlands. In recent times, the village has expanded to accommodate some of the workers from nearby Sellafield. The Wheatsheaf stands beside the road junction in the centre of the old village, with its cottage-like exterior facing the morning sun. The decorative flower baskets in the summer complement well the low-beamed interior which has been welcoming the traveller for 200 years and more.

There should be little difficulty in finding food to satisfy here. Snacks include sandwiches, filled potatoes and toasties, whilst a good range of main meals is offered. Liver and bacon is not the common meal it once was and it is a pleasant change to find it on the menu with a variety of steak, sausage and fish dishes. Vegetarians might start with garlic mushrooms before their cannelloni. Food is served from 12 noon to 2 pm and 6 pm to 9 pm. A children's choice is available.

Bar hours are from 12 noon to 11 pm (10.30 pm on Sundays), though it is wise to check winter afternoon closing times. A freehouse, Bass, Fuller's London Pride and Worthington BB beers are on draught. Stouts are Guinness and Caffrey's, the ciders are Strongbow and Dry Blackthorn and lagers are Tennents and Grolsch. Families are most welcome, but please ask before taking your dog inside. A pleasant, shaded patio from which you can watch the world go by is next to the road.

Telephone: 019467 25821.

How to get there: Turn into the village from the A595. The pub is beside the central T-junction.

Parking: A free public car park is across the road, 50 yards in the Wasdale direction.

Length of the walk: 3¼ miles. Map: OS Landranger 89 West Cumbria (pub GR 067035).

Gosforth holds some of the most famous relics of Viking times in the north. The walk gives an opportunity to see these, combined with a circuit through the farmland of the narrow coastal plain and up towards the fell edge for some fine views. Except after heavy rain, most of the route should be reasonably dry underfoot. There is one short climb.

The Walk

Turn round to the right from the pub door and take the Millom road past Gosforth Gate (1628 and once the library) and a row of wooden-clad houses on the left. At the A595 cross over with care and walk down the verge of the B5344 past the hotel, then cross to the left-hand side at the entrance of Haverigg Moorside. Take the stile just inside to the right (there is no sign) and cross over a small field to a second stile – notice the pigeon loft over the barn as you go. Turn to the left on the track now and walk through the fields between high banks. At the top of the brow the view is all round. Almost behind are the towers of Sellafield, to the right the Isle of Man sits low on the horizon, and ahead is Black Combe, while to the left are the fells around lower Wasdale and Blengdale. Continue to the gate on the right before the track ends and walk to the right, down to the stile in the bottom corner of the field. Follow the right-hand boundary of the next field to a further stile and turn to the left on the far side. Walk through to the main road gate beside the hedge, keeping a small plantation clearly to your right.

Cross back over the main road, again with care, and go right for 30 yards along the wood side to the path to the left beside the sports field of Harecroft Hall school, the Victorian buildings of which you can see between the beech trees. The view at the far side of the field just extends to the lower end of the famous Wasdale screes below Whin Rigg. Use the iron kissing-gate in the corner and cross the next field to a footbridge, taking the gate in the corner onto a farm track. Continue ahead on a clear

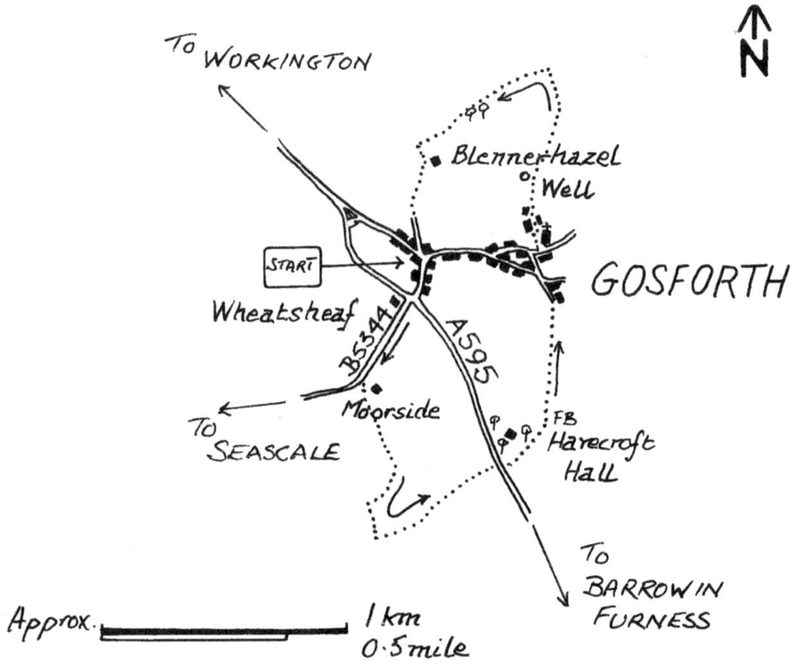

path between a hedge to the right and a fence to the left and walk through Fell View mobile home park. At the '5 mph' sign go straight ahead on the old path past the Mountain Rescue post in the old barn.

Bear to the left at the Wasdale road (the Horse and Groom pub is just along to the right) and cross over in 50 yards to the lane which runs up beside Whitecross House (1857) and past the school. At the junction go right and left and into St Mary's churchyard. The tall and slender shaft of the red sandstone Viking cross stands beside the south gate. It was carved with stories from the sagas, including that of the world ash tree, Yggdrasil, and erected here sometime in the middle of the 10th century. Two tombstones and part of a former frieze inside the church are also carved with Viking legends. The church, as it stands, is basically 14th century on an earlier Norman foundation. It may, unfortunately, be locked. To the rear, brand new parish rooms have recently been built in total keeping with the old buildings. Leave by the west gate, at the tower end, and turn to the right towards Gosforth Hall (dated 1658), a hotel, and go between it and the, oddly named, red sandstone Pine Lodge and through the white gate at the top of the car park. Continue ahead, passing a garden with a pool and conservatory, to a stile. Keep to the right-hand boundary beside an old walled pond and, at the corner, walk ahead up the rushy field to a stile just right of an old iron fence. Inside this enclosure is a former holy well, now covered over. There is a suggestion of the existence of a stone building, probably a chapel, having been there in the past.

Take the stile immediately to the right of the well and climb steeply up next to the right-hand cobblestoned bank for a short distance. Turn left immediately through the gate onto an old banked track guarded by thorn trees. In summer the bracken grows thickly and fallen cobbles make for a short length of difficult ground underfoot. Just to the right of the next stile is the unusual sight of a laburnum tree in the hedgerow. Continue on more or less the same line (not to the left) and go through a stone squeeze stile to cross a track by a small wood of beeches on the left. Pass the gate on the left and, at the next stile, turn down the track to the left and drop down to Blennerhazel. Swing right on the access track in front of the wall and go down through the trees to the village. The pub is 20 yards to the left.

5 Calder Bridge
The Stanley Arms Hotel

Calder is a common northern name, indicating a rocky or rapid river. By the time it has reached Calder Bridge this one has become wider and smoother and swirls over flat beds of sandstone below the gardens of the Stanley Arms (named for the Stanleys of Ponsonby Hall, now Pelham House) on its short way to the sea. The hotel's buildings are based around a 17th-century coaching inn with later additions, the restaurant once being the stabling. The inside has the high-ceilinged elegance associated here, as so often elsewhere, with what was expected by those who could afford to travel in style some 300 years ago. It is family-run and exudes a welcoming and comfortable feel as a result.

The service of food is from 11 am to 3 pm and 5.30 pm to the amazingly late 11 pm (9 pm on Sundays). There is an unusually good range of starters, including an interesting variation on my mother's cheese and onions (a simple but luscious combination!) – this one in a pancake. The numerous main courses are excellent value and freshly prepared with a better vegetarian range than many. Snacks, a children's choice and a daily sweets board are available.

The bar hours are from 11 am to 11 pm (10.30 pm on Sundays). This freehouse offers Jennings, Boddingtons and Whitbread beers, with

Murphy's stout, Heineken and Fürstenburg lagers and Strongbow cider. The gardens overlook the river, and a family area is set aside by the garden door. Dogs are welcome if on leads.

Telephone: 01946 841235.

How to get there: The hotel is at the side of the main A595 coast road, south of Egremont.

Parking: At the side and rear of the hotel, but please check at the bar before leaving your car while you walk. There is also public parking beside the village hall, next to the garage up the lane beyond the church.

Length of the walk: 4 miles, or just under 4½ miles if you take the alternative route (marked 'A' on the sketch map). Map: OS Landranger 89 West Cumbria (hotel GR 043059).

The valley of the river Calder is as tucked away now as it ever was. The walk passes the ruins of the former Cistercian abbey and continues up the valley through delightful woodlands. The circuit is completed through open farmland and green lanes. The short alternative route may require you getting your feet wet.

The Walk

Bear right from the hotel, cross the main road bridge and walk through the churchyard. The church of St Bridget is a pleasant red sandstone, mid-Victorian building in earlier style, which glows in sunshine (sadly, it is usually kept locked these days). Exit up the steps and turn to the right. Ignore the immediate footpath but go 5 yards further and turn right again, up the track past the garage and the car repair shop with the toilets behind in an old stone shed. The route is still known as the Monks Road and passes through Mill Farm to an up and over stile, then following the left-hand boundary towards the buildings around Calder Abbey. The far bank of the river is heavily wooded and buzzards often glide overhead. Take the gate to the left by the first stone shed and continue to a stile in the corner behind the row of stone cottages.

The driveway is the entrance to Calder Abbey. This is open between Friday and Tuesday from 10 am to 6 pm. It is privately owned and there is a charge. Founded in 1134 as a Savignac abbey, it became Cistercian in 1148. It was soon nearly destroyed by a Scottish raid and the monks fled to Furness. Refused permission to stay there, they moved on to Byland in North Yorkshire. Calder was re-settled from Furness in 1180. The ruins are almost entirely 13th century and stand to a considerable height, as can be seen over the fence at the far side of the driveway. Much was incorporated into a symmetrical Georgian country house of 1770. The

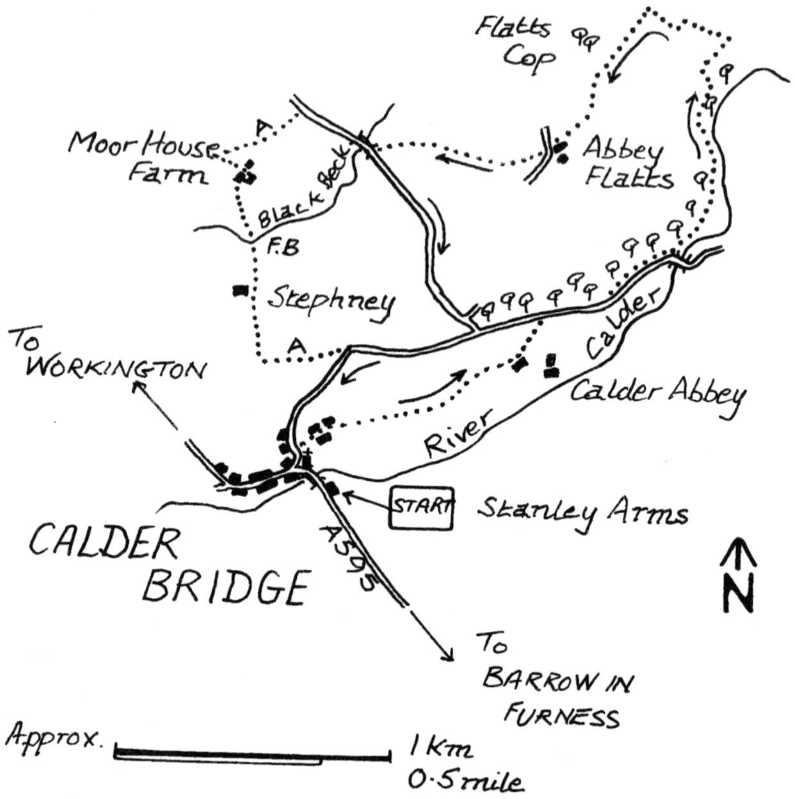

poet Samuel Taylor Coleridge was here on his walking tour of 1802 and later, Harriet Martineau, the 19th-century social reformer, wrote appreciatively of the very hotel from which your walk began and of the quiet scene in the valley.

Walk forward over the driveway beside the iron fence and amongst nettles before passing some fine large lime trees beside the lane. Turn to the right and continue round the curve of the valley. At the bend there is a stone-built underpass which links the fields on either side. Walk beyond the two stone sheds in the field on the right and take the stile to the left into the wood. There is a good view half-right to Wheel Fell. You are now on a permissive path, parallel to the lane, within the National Park Access Area of Calder Woods. Follow the path forward until you reach the track just in from the river bridge, where you turn left. Go by the old mill house, down to the right beside the river, and in 50 yards bear up left and walk through fine mixed woodlands of oak, sycamore, beech, rowan, hazel, elder, holly, ash, birch and the occasional pine. The woodland floor is lush with fern and woodrush but gradually changes to become fine heathland grasses. The path climbs up through the wood to exit to a field by a stile alongside a piece of sandstone wall. Go right along the boundary on an old, worn track, and swing round the head of a ghyll to pass a water trough. Both black and white thorn bloom on the bank and overhang the two stiles in the corner. Drop steeply into, and out of, a ghyll to climb to a third stile.

Turn left across the runnel and follow the line of the old boundary marked by oak trees to find the stile in the corner of the field to the left, by the gate. At the next gate go through and turn left along the boundary amongst gorse, passing the telegraph pole. On the brow is the clump of trees on a low knoll known as Flatts Cop. The path goes through the left-hand corner of the field but you may find the minor detour to the nearby steel gate more sensible. The view ahead is to the towers of Sellafield and out to sea. Return to the left-hand boundary and walk forward to pick up the old track (ignore the new tractor track), between hedges, which leads down to the lane beside the buildings of Abbey Flatts Farm and its pot-bellied pig. Cross over the road, out of the National Park, and go through the gate (there is no sign), following the green track. At the two gates the path uses the right-hand one and follows the left-hand boundary down to a gate to the lane. This patch can be very wet for a few yards. At the lane, turn to the left and follow it, bearing right at junctions, to return to the village.

Alternatively (marked 'A' on the sketch map), go right and along the lane to the track to the left for Moor House Farm. Pass the modern bungalow to the double gates on the left and go ahead to the farm buildings. In the yard, go to the right by the house and take the steel gate to the field directly ahead. Bear along the left-hand boundary on its stone dyke to find the location of the footbridge 50 yards right of the field corner. (At the time of writing the bridge had not yet been replaced after being washed away in a flood. Under normal conditions it is perfectly possible to step onto the gravel of the beck and up the other bank.) Walk ahead to the buildings of Stephney and go into the yard and out again by the asbestos-roofed barn. The path goes through the gate ahead and crosses the field right of the small copse to exit to a green lane. Bear left and walk along to the metalled lane to the village. The view up the valley is a wide one. At the junction, turn right to descend to the village and the hotel.

6 Ennerdale Bridge
The Shepherd's Arms Hotel

The bridge spans the river Ehen at the point where the routes from the valley meet those of the coastal plain. In the past this was an area of mining activity but all that has gone and today this is the largest of the western Lakeland valleys with no motor road, and the upper valley didn't get its electricity until 1989. The Shepherd's Arms Hotel is a traditional building, tucked in amongst the other houses of the village. Although well served with modern facilities, open log fires still blaze in the winter and the aim, all year round, is comfort.

The restaurant specialises in game and home-smoked salmon whilst the bar menu has a very definite West Cumbrian tinge amongst more standard fare. Rollmop herrings can be followed by lamb chops with Cumberland sauce, or home-made soup complemented by a pie of wild rabbit and bacon – either is a mouth-watering prospect! Children's portions are served and there is a vegetarian menu. The restaurant is a non-smoking area. Service is from 12.30 pm to 2 pm and from 7 pm to 8.30 pm.

The standard beer is Worthington and this is supplemented by a range of guest beers such as Bateman XB and XXXB. The draught lager is Carlsberg. The bar is open all day, every day, from 11 am to 11 pm (10.30 pm on Sundays). There is a pleasant beer garden to the rear. Dogs are

welcome, except in the restaurant. Accommodation is available.
Telephone: 01946 861249.

How to get there: Turn off the A5086 Egremont to Cockermouth road at Cleator Moor or, from further north, approach via Kirkland. The hotel is in the northern part of the village, just below the school.

Parking: At the hotel and by the roadside in the village. An alternative would be to make the hotel the halfway point of your walk and park in the front car park near the lake at GR 085153.

Length of the walk: 5½ miles. Map: OS Landranger 89 West Cumbria (hotel GR 069159).

Lower Ennerdale is readily accessible but the upper valley, below Pillar and Kirk Fell, would require a considerable walk. The views into the fells from the route are fine indeed and a longish length of the path follows the lake shore. There are no significant climbs.

The Walk

Go straight ahead from the hotel doorway and bear round beside the school, which takes up most of the triangular green. (To the right, and over the bridge, is the rather unprepossessing church which inspired Wordsworth to write his poem *The Two Brothers.*) Go left on the lane and walk along past Low Moor End to the fork at the corner of the plantations. Turn right here and walk beside the larches, past the white cottages, to the next corner. Continue straight ahead past Gryke Cottage and, in 150 yards, pass a further cottage on the left to a stile and footbridge over the swift flowing river Ehen, overhung with alder, willow and rowan. The track goes beside a very unhappy looking plantation of pines. Turn to the left, up the valley, at the T-junction of tracks at the base of the fell and work your way along between plantations and fields. Down to the left is what appears to be a new farm building in traditional stone – it is, in fact, a water treatment works. As you pass the house amongst the sycamores on the left a view opens up of the lower lake across to the plantations around Bowness Knott and the bulk of Herdus, behind. It was these, and the more extensive plantings further up the valley, which caused such a great outcry in the 1930s against what was seen as despoliation of the scene. The outcome was an agreement for no further plantations of conifers in the central fells of the Lake District and the controversy undoubtedly sowed the seeds for the much more sensitive landscape policies which have evolved in more recent times.

Continue on via a small iron gate and a stile to a ford of the beck beside the lakeshore. Turn sharply to the left and walk to the footbridge across

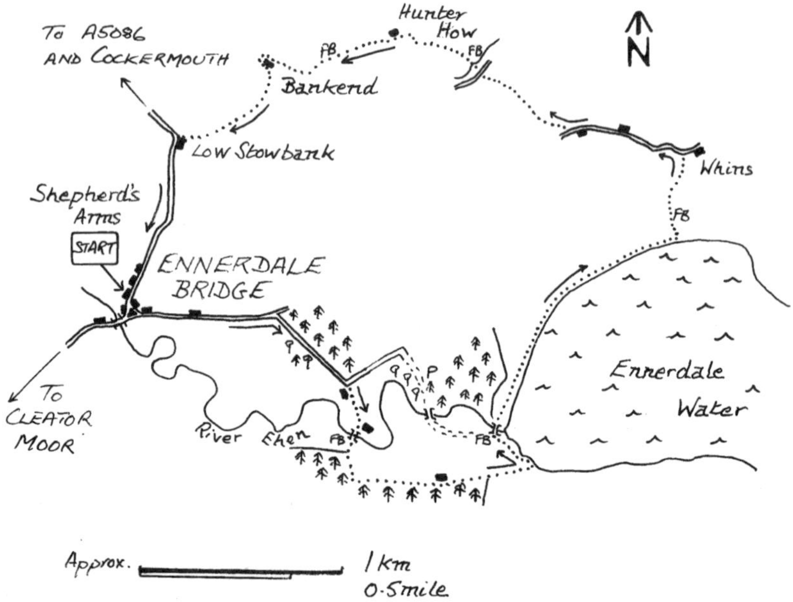

the outlet of the lake. (The forest car park is about 300 yards to the left and across the river.) The path continues along the shore, passing a Scout camp in the trees to the left and with a fine view up to Angler's Crag on the right. The famous rock climbing routes, at the head of the valley, are tucked out of sight beyond. Bracken and gorse straggle along the shore and a resident flock of greylag geese graze on the grass sward. (This whole area was threatened once again, in the late 1970s, with plans to raise the lake level to enable greater water abstraction – luckily, these were successfully fought.) Enter National Trust land through an iron gate and walk ahead, past the track from the left by an informal car park, and past the 'private road' sign to the next gate and kissing-gate. Some 20 yards beyond, bear back to the left on a faint path across a rather wet area to an up and over stile hidden amongst the gorse. On the far side, bear right and climb the rushy field beside a little beck and pass the wall corner. There is a footbridge and stile to the right where the fence starts. Follow the old track along the stoned dyke and hedge line to the lane by a green barn close to the Whins.

Go left along the lane between high hedges covered in a scramble of vetch, goosegrass and bramble and with unusual masses of yellow pimpernel in places in summer. Pass the track right to Croftfoot and take a final view back to the lake from the brow top. Continue past Howside, ignoring the footpath almost opposite. Turn right on the next path in 20 yards and bear slightly left along the old hedge line down a wet field to find a new gate on the left of the bank. Go through and continue along the right-hand boundary on the same line to the far bottom right and go through the gap. Take the stile on the left and follow the right-hand boundary, cutting across the corner to a stile onto a lane. Cross a few paces right to a stile and a footbridge by a ford over the Croasdale beck. You exit the National Park at this point.

Pass the fence corner on the left and follow the faint track in a dog-leg towards Hunter How, then follow the arrow through the buildings to the gate opposite Hunter How itself. Go through and take the stile immediately to the right over the fence. Cross through the dampish overgrowth of meadowsweet to the faint line of the path along the far boundary. Seek its rather illogical progress to a footbridge and two stiles in the far right-hand corner of the field. Bear diagonally left to the gate in the far corner and cross towards the buildings of Bankend. Exit to the lane and pass the house to the footpath sign to the left (when I last passed this way there was no stile to make crossing the fence easy). The path goes back behind the house and swings round the green knoll on the lower route, eventually crossing through the fields to the lane on the right of the buildings of Low Stowbank. Take care as you walk round the corner to the left and use the often orchid-rich verge to return to the village and the hotel.

7 Sandwith
The Dog and Partridge

The village of Sandwith (pronounced 'Sanith') lies tucked in the shallow valley which runs between the town of Whitehaven and the village of St Bees. Modern main roads bypass it and the broad street is as busy with Coast to Coast walkers (at the start or the end of their journey) as it is with other traffic. The Dog and Partridge stands on the corner at the top of the village and displays its tidy and business-like face to the world. In years gone by it was a customs-bonded warehouse, but such days are long past.

Food is available between 12 noon and 2 pm on Wednesdays, Thursdays, Fridays and Sundays and from 6.30 pm to 9 pm each evening. A special feature is made of Thursday, which is steak night and is particularly busy – it is wise to book. In an effort to fit the food to the location, my own lunchtime choice here would be the home-made soup, followed by deep fried scampi, but you could, with equal pleasure, choose filled jacket potatoes, for example, or sandwiches. There is a special children's menu.

As a freehouse, the Dog and Partridge stocks Jennings, Bass, Stones and Worthington beers. Lager is Tennents, cider is Dry Blackthorn and the stouts are both Guinness and Caffrey's. The bar is open from 12 noon to 3 pm and from 6.30 pm to 11 pm (10.30 pm on Sundays). Customers are welcome to consume their own food outside in the beer garden when they purchase drinks. Please ask prior to bringing your dog inside.

Telephone: 01946 692671.

How to get there: The B5345 links Whitehaven and St Bees. From Whitehaven approach Sandwith via Kells or Wilson Pit Road, or from St Bees go through Rottington.

Parking: At the pub and by the roadside.

Length of the walk: 4½ miles. Map: OS Landranger 89 West Cumbria (pub GR 965149).

The cliffs of St Bees (at about 300 ft) are far and away the highest between North Wales and the far west coast of Scotland and are, uniquely, made of soft red sandstone. Much of the total of about 4 miles (of which the route includes 2 or so) is a Royal Society for the Protection of Birds reserve, which has unrestricted access. In season the flowers are also superb. The views are wide and open.

Warning: Care should, of course, be taken on the cliffs. Heed the notices!

The Walk

Pass down the street by red sandstone cottages, some of them very small indeed, and newly converted barns to the first turn to the right and its sign, 'C2C' (for the Coast to Coast walk devised by that famous writer of Lakeland, and other, guidebooks, Alfred Wainwright). Turn up the lane, with its profusion of growth on high banks, and continue as far as the bend by the tall mast on the left. Go to the right and take the track downwards, towards the cliffs, amongst gorse, whinberry, blackberry, cinquefoil and heathland grasses with a variety of butterflies at the right time of year. The view across the Solway Firth is to the Isle of Whithorn and Criffel, and the chimneys of the chemical works on the edge of Whitehaven town are to the right. Go through the final red-soiled field (of oats when I last passed) along the right-hand boundary of stone and turf dyke with hawkbit, woodsage, scabious and foxgloves.

Turn to the left along the cliff path. There is a cool breeze off the sea at all seasons – even on the hottest of days. Hard back, you can see the mole of Whitehaven harbour. The clear path wanders along the clifftop with massive blocks of detached sandstone scattered down below and a half-formed stack separated from the cliff face. Heather, harebells and yellow gorse bloom beside the way. At a clear groove in the rocks a collection of graffiti has been carved by young lovers, the (not very) idle, and vandals – take your own choice of explanation. It has certainly been going on since

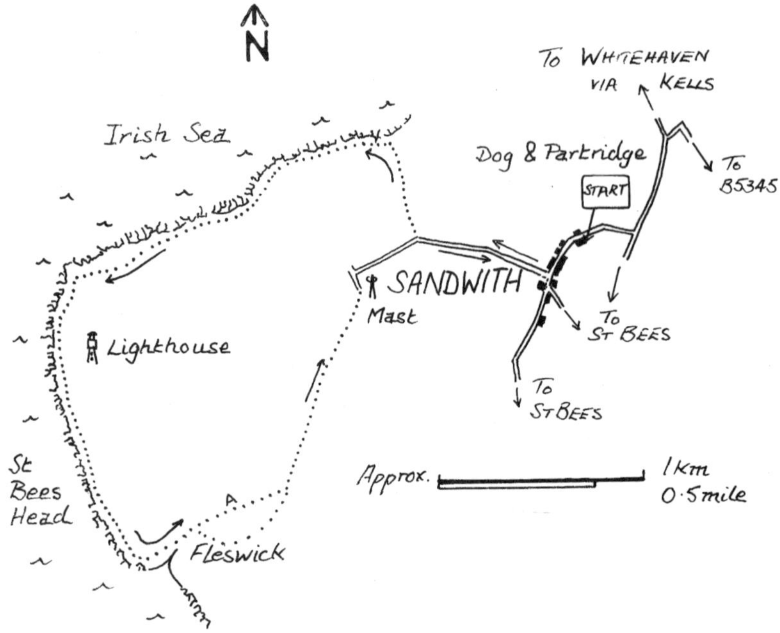

1916! A few steps further will bring you to the boundary of the RSPB reserve.

Stay up above the field won from a bench of the cliff and reach an 'Open Access' area under the Countryside Stewardship Scheme. Aim across the short, grazed turf to the left-hand stile and on to the stile in the corner. Continue along the clifftop. The white hut below the lighthouse is the old coastguard station. A lighthouse was first built here in 1717 and the present one has been in existence since 1866. There is an RSPB warning sign about the cliffs being dangerous. In a couple of places you will find stiles into carefully railed areas from which you can safely watch the seabirds in flight, and at rest and nesting (the height of the season is June) on the narrow cliff ledges. Fulmars, kittiwakes and other gulls, guillemots (including England's only breeding black guillemots) and razorbills can be seen. In several areas the turf by the clifftop is deep enough for the burrows of puffins. Over the sea you may see gannets, shearwaters and eider ducks. Eventually swing a little left and drop steeply down towards the gash of Fleswick (say 'flezzick' – perhaps the bay of flesh or meat?) and its small, pebbly beach and shelves of red rock, with patches of flowers clinging on precariously.

Return to the head of the gulley, where there is a rough seat beside a green track through a gate. The formal path goes right to the line of the bank up the slope and up its left-hand side, then swings across the field to its top left-hand corner. Since this will, almost certainly, involve walking over ploughed land the alternative (marked 'A' on the sketch map) is to use the stile just right of the seat and go up the bank side on the informal path to reach the same point at the crest, where there is a large up and over stile. The view from the top is all round – Whitehaven, the village and the high fells of the Lake District. The mixture of arable land and the lush banks makes this a place where yellowhammers still chirr their 'little bit of bread and no chee-eeze' in the hot summer sun. Turn to the left along the green track and follow through three up and over stiles to reach the lighthouse lane below the mast again. Return down the lane to the village.

Close by, and worth visiting, is St Bees. The almost complete Norman church is what is left of the priory. This, the story goes, was founded by Irish St Bega who came with her nuns in the middle of the 7th century and begged ground of the local lord for a place to settle. He agreed to give as much ground as snow should cover on Midsummer day – and, lo and behold, it snowed (no one who lives permanently in the shadow of the Lakeland mountains will be all that surprised!) The independent school, founded by Archbishop Grindal of Canterbury in 1583, still flourishes though the Theological College (1816–1866) which once accompanied it is long closed. For anyone interested in industrial archaeology or maritime history, Whitehaven will also be a must. The museum illustrates both aspects.

8 Buttermere
The Fish Hotel

The village (hamlet really) of Buttermere and the Fish itself are famous. Before the motor age the valley of Buttermere and Crummock was fairly inaccessible and Nicholas Size's novel *The Secret Valley*, takes this as the key in a tale of our Norse ancestors. In the beck, by the Bridge Hotel, can be seen the site of the waterwheel of the mill. This may have been built in those far-off days and was thus, perhaps, the oldest in Britain. Melvyn Bragg's more recent novel *The Maid of Buttermere*, retells the tale (the outline is true at any rate) of Mary, the attractive daughter of the landlord of the Fish, who was conned into a bigamous marriage. She was, herself, a tourist attraction and Coleridge, De Quincey and Wordsworth all wrote about her. Ever since travellers first came to admire Lakeland, Buttermere has been a deservedly popular spot, so much so now that at the main holiday times parking can be hard to find. The Fish Hotel is at the bottom of the short lane by the Mill (Sail) beck bridge, a post box in the wall marking the corner. It has been there since the 1700s and has been in the present family ownership for many years.

Lunchtime and evening menus for the bar are extensive. Food is served from 12 noon to 2 pm and 6 pm to 9 pm each day. In this setting, my own inclination is to settle for the substantial ploughman's lunch, but a

Cumberland sausage could be even more filling – or you could take a wholemeal bread sandwich as a snack and return for the evening steaks. The latter course of action would give you a chance to indulge in the iced-brandy meringue for afters!

The bar of this freehouse carries Theakston Old Peculier, XB and BB plus Younger Scotch ale and a couple of guest beers. Stout is Murphy's, lagers are Beck's, Coors and McEwan's and ciders are Dry Blackthorn and Cidermaster. Opening hours are from 10.30 am to 3 pm and 6 pm to 11 pm (10.30 pm on Sundays). There is a pleasant beer garden. Dog owners should note that their pets are not permitted on the premises. Overnight accommodation is available if you have time for a longer stay.

Telephone: 017687 70253.

How to get there: The low routes are from Cockermouth on the B5292 and the B5289, and from the A5086 in the west via Mockerkin and Loweswater; intermediate are from the A66, at Braithwaite, via Newlands (which is narrow) or via Whinlatter and Lorton on the B5292 (which is longer); the most dramatic is from Keswick, via Borrowdale, and over the Honister Pass.

Parking: At the pub or in the adjacent National Park car park. Alternatively, park at Gatesgarth, at the head of the lake, and visit the Fish at the halfway point.

Length of the walk: 4 miles. Map: OS Landranger 89 West Cumbria (hotel GR 174169).

If, for whatever reason, you don't have the time for walking amongst the high fells, or this is not a practicable proposition for you, then a circuit of Buttermere is a very fine substitute – it gets close to some of the highest and wildest summits, gives magnificent views from lake level and is easy going underfoot. Buttermere is the second smallest of the main lakes in the Lake District (only nearby Loweswater is smaller). Sadly, the closure of the short tunnel on the shore path by Dalegarth precludes this being an almost totally flat and dry route at all times.

The Walk

Turn down the track beside the car park of the hotel. Even as you reach the bend the first of many superlative views is before you (there simply are no ordinary, everyday words which describe adequately the panoramas of summit, fell, ghyll, wood and lake which you can see at all seasons in this valley). Half-right is a glimpse of Crummock Water – the bigger of the two lakes, in fact – and a view of the path up towards Mosedale and of the great shoulder of Mellbreak. Turn up and across the valley now and take

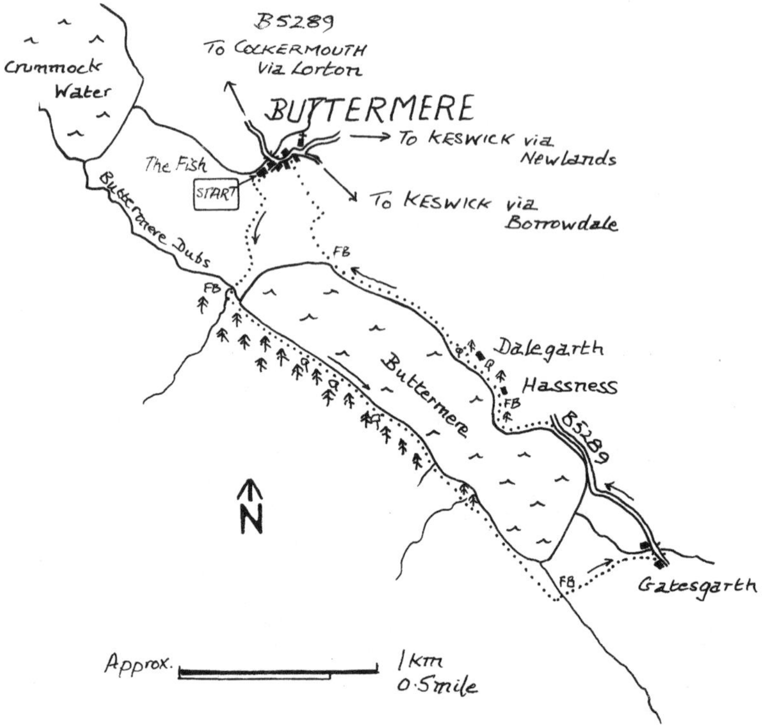

the left-hand path for Sour Milk Ghyll, which tumbles down between the trees in front of you from Bleaberry Tarn, hidden under the crags between High Stile and Red Pike. (Scale Force, about a mile and a quarter along the right-hand path, has the greatest single drop of any fall in the Lake District at 120 ft.) Enter National Trust land and take either the shore path or the inner one to the footbridge over Buttermere Dubs.

Turn left, up the valley, on a very clear permissive path by the shore (NOT up to the right), and walk along through the oak, rowan, alder, sycamore and some fine larch in Burtness Wood, where the woodland floor has a thick carpet of mosses in places. The view is now up the lake towards Fleetwith Pike at the lake head, with the valley to the left, which leads to the Honister Pass between it and Robinson Crags. Further along the path there are gaps through the trees on the shore of the lake and the view back is to the village, with Whiteless Pike immediately behind it and Grasmoor beyond. The occasional sweet chestnut tree stands by the path.

Eventually you emerge from the wood, more or less opposite the two large houses of Dalegarth and Hassness, on the shore below Goat Crag on the far side of the lake. Cross over the beck flowing out of the hanging valley of Burtness Combe, and pass the clump of larch on the left to meet the path which comes down from the right from Scarth Gap. Cross the footbridge to the left and walk over the green fields, which contrast so strongly in autumn with the russet of the bracken of the fell sides. The valley to the right of Fleetwith Pike, Warnscale Bottom, is now in full view, with the jagged ridge of Haystacks towering over it (it was here that the ashes of that great Lakeland aficionado Alfred Wainwright were scattered). At the farm, join the road and turn across the bridge towards the village. There is often an ice-cream van here, by the car park, and the sheep have quickly learned to tease impatient motorists and entertain camera-clicking tourists.

From the top of the brow you can see right into the hanging valley of Burtness Combe, back across the the lake. Drop down to the edge of the water, where the road is at its narrowest, and take the signed path to the left; a little further takes you to an unsigned track which avoids the short rocky section past old hollies and birches. Drop down a little again to a path over fields and swing round with the shore to come to the large pines at the bottom of the woods around Hassness. Many of their roots have been washed out by the wind-blown waves beating on the shore, and the tuna-coloured upper bark glows when there is late afternoon sun. A footbridge takes you into the wood proper and in amongst beeches to a path which zig-zags up to the right to avoid the collapsing tunnel on the shore. This is a short and steep section which is, if anything, rather more awkward as you descend on the far side of the bluff – take care! You can see the blocked-off tunnel from the little beach. Continue along the shore through parkland trees and then the thin woodland on Pike Rigg. Once more there is a good view across to the ridge on the far side of the lake.

At the end of the wood, beyond the lake end, is another footbridge. Follow the fence round to join up with the footpath coming in from the right from Bowderbeck. Turn left and drop a little through the field to go into the farmyard of Wilkinsyke, with a red sandstone arch over the barn door to the right. Exit onto the road across from the tiny church of St James (1841) and the parish rooms, in the old school, on the bank opposite and go left and left again to return to the Fish. You might care to note that the local show – a good one – is held towards the end of October.

9 Embleton
The Wheatsheaf Inn

This has remained gentle farming country since the day when Eanbald first thought to establish his farm here 1,000 years ago, close by where his Celtic predecessors had already settled. The village straggles along the old main road into Cockermouth town from the east and doesn't really have a centre. The Wheatsheaf stands opposite the minute post office, its frontage facing south towards Ling Fell. At some point the inside has been given a face-lift which, happily, has left it looking good and the L-shaped bar is a welcoming spot.

The bar menu offers a goodly choice to the walker. Light meals include sandwiches, filled potatoes, toasties and a selection of omelettes – which makes a pleasing change. More substantial meals are also available. The home-made pies are well known around about. Both vegetarians and children are catered for too. Food is served from 12 noon to 2 pm and from 6 pm (7 pm on Sundays) to 9 pm in the evening.

This is a Jennings pub (the brewery is just along the road in Cockermouth) and offers their own bitter as well as the delightful Cocker Hoop and guest ales. Stouts are Guinness and Murphy's, the lagers are Stella Artois and Heineken and the cider is Dry Blackthorn. Bar times are 12 noon to 2.30 pm (3 pm on Saturdays and Sundays) and 6 pm to 11 pm

(7 pm to 10.30 pm on Sundays). The beer garden gives a fine view over the valley and there is also a family area in the dining room, upstairs.
Telephone: 017687 76408.

How to get there: Turn at any of the signs from the A66. You will find the pub on the upper side of the road.

Parking: There is a large car park behind the pub.

Length of the walk: 3 miles Map: OS Landranger 89 West Cumbria (pub GR 173305).

The main A66 apart, this is a quiet corner of the National Park. The walk crosses the shallow valley, with some pleasant views to east and south, and uses some of the old green roads. Halfway round the circuit is one of the most remarkable museums in the North of England.

The Walk

Go from the pub door over the road to the post office and turn to walk past the telephone box, bearing down to the right beyond Rakefoot Cottages. Drop down the short brow to the village hall and the field to the left where Highland cattle graze. Cross over the A66 with great care. Turn immediately right along the access to Low and High Netherscale. Just inside the gate of the latter is a footbridge to the left and an up and over stile. Stay between the left-hand boundary and the ranch fencing (there will probably be horses in the field) and duck below overhanging hawthorns to reach a stile on the left into a little plantation of conifers. Go over and pass to the left, below the garden wall, to a stile onto the access track. Use the steel gate ahead to go along the bridleway under the telegraph poles, swinging slowly to the far right-hand corner of the field and a narrow extension leading to an old green track between overgrown hedges.

At the T-junction, turn to the right on the old road of Seacross Lonning. Its hedges are rich with holly, hazel, blackthorn, hawthorn, rowan, roses and the occasional lime tree. Walk ahead the length of two and a half fields on your left-hand side to a steel gate on the left with double hooks. Turn through it, up the slope, on an old sunken track (there is no sign) along the left-hand boundary as far as the wooden gate. Go through this to the far side of the boundary line and continue up towards the buildings of Low Abbey. On the far side of the gate, go left on the lower track and pass in front of the old farmhouse, swinging round by a little walled garden to a small gate into the bottom of a wood. Proceed through to walk in front of the house at High Abbey to a small gate beside the water trough and pump. Continue ahead, with the old hedge and wall on your left and the

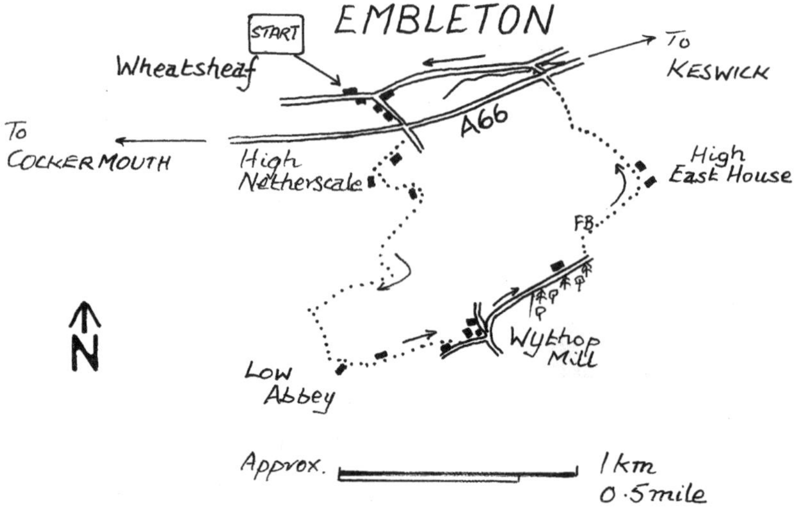

view to Sale Fell directly before you. Half-back is the nick by Slate Fell which carries the old road into Cockermouth. Cross the stile and fence and walk below the house gardens to an iron gate to the right. Pass through and keep tight beside the cypress hedge on your left to a stile on to the lane at the end of the garden.

Walk down left to the bridge over Wythop (pronounced Widdup) beck and bear left to the Wythop Mill museum. This was, unusually, a water-powered sawmill with an overshot wheel, and houses a unique collection of old wood-working tools and displays about the locality, including, for instance, the salt spring at Stanger, at the far end of the parish, close to the river Cocker. Opening times are at weekends in March and then every day except Monday from Easter to October. There is also a coffee shop and restaurant. It was close to the mill that a Celtic sword with a jewelled hilt was found, of 1st-century date, now in the British Museum.

Return from the mill to the bridge and turn sharp left along the lane. Pass the entrance of Wadcrag and go left down the steps on the footpath beyond the big Scots pine trees. Follow the right-hand boundary of the field to a stile and a footbridge and then keep to the left-hand boundary. At the buildings of High East House join the access lane and walk along it to the A66. Cross directly over, looking out for speeding traffic. Go over the bridge across the Dubwath beck and turn left upstream along the verge of the road. Enter the village by the massive modern storage sheds in the lower part of Seathwaite How quarries, which operated from 1907 to 1950 and employed as many as 80 men at one time. Join the footway past the Wesleyan chapel (1863), now a house, and return to the pub.

10 Bassenthwaite
The Castle Inn Hotel

The Castle Inn Hotel, which is linked to the Best Western chain, has gradually developed over the years to a substantial hotel and conference centre with an excellent and well-patronised bar. The core was a farmhouse and the building extensions have been carefully blended into it. The poet Thomas Gray (of *Elegy in a Country Churchyard* fame) dined here in 1769 – a very early tourist and a great promoter of the 'terrific' scenery of the Lakes. The hotel stands beside an almost crossroads about a mile from Bassenthwaite village itself. The name of the village and of the lake (the only lake in the Lake District – all the others are called mere or water; curiously, it used to be known as Broadwater) seems to derive from an odd mixture of a Norman-French nickname (Bastun – referring, perhaps, to someone who was 'as thin as a lath') and the old Norse for a clearing in the forest.

Meals are available from 12 noon to 2 pm and 6 pm (7 pm on Sundays) to 9 pm each day. Snacks include sandwiches and a better-than-average choice of burger. The full-meal selection is mostly from the specials board and there are a few regulars, starters and main courses. The offering of Cumberland sausage and black pudding with potatoes and salad would certainly suit me on any cold winter day. There is a separate children's menu.

The bar is open from 11.30 am to 3 pm and 5.30 pm to 11 pm on weekdays and Saturdays, and from 12 noon to 3 pm and 7 pm to 10.30 pm on Sundays. The range of draught ales reflects the choice you would expect of a large freehouse. Jennings Bitter and Cumberland Ale are joined by Courage Directors, Webster's Yorkshire Bitter and Beamish on draught. You will also find Guinness, Foster's and Kronenbourg lagers and Strongbow cider. There is a patio area, and a garden beside the hotel. Families are particularly welcome in the lounge, and children are allowed in the bar areas until 9 pm. Dogs are not permitted.

Telephone: 017687 76401.

How to get there: The hotel is at the junction of the B5291 (linking with the A66) and the A591 between Keswick and the A595 (Carlisle road).

Parking: A large car park is located at the hotel and there is some additional parking across the road.

Length of the walk: 3¾ miles, or 5¾ miles if you take the alternative route along part of the eastern side of the lake. Map: OS Landranger 89 West Cumbria (hotel GR 215327).

The route of the walk commences in the upper valley of the river Derwent, which drains Bassenthwaite Lake. The lake itself belongs to the National Park Authority. There is an opportunity to visit the farm, country sports and riding facilities close to Armathwaite Hall. You can return along the end of the lake or take the optional extension (one section of this is extremely boggy in wet weather), which gets you closer to some of the shore and has excellent views of the western flanks of Skiddaw.

The Walk

Walk along the frontage of the hotel and down the right-hand verge of the B5291 for 250 yards to a bridleway on the right (just before the old toll-bar cottage). Before you turn, enjoy a first view up the valley towards the head of the lake, with Wythop Woods and Thornthwaite Forest on the Lorton Fells to the right. Pass the County Council road depot on the right and a triangle of woodland on your left and continue on the track to cross over the Coal beck. Take the path immediately on the right by the gate into the Forest Enterprise woodland of Messengermire Wood. The path swings and gently rises up the contours of the side of the hill amongst some fine middle-aged beech trees. Exit to a field and go over to the ruin of Lingeybank. As you cross, the view opens to the ridge of Setmurthy Common, on the far side of the Derwent, with its Iron Age remains on Elva Hill.

At Lingeybank turn to the left and drop down the stony track, with a

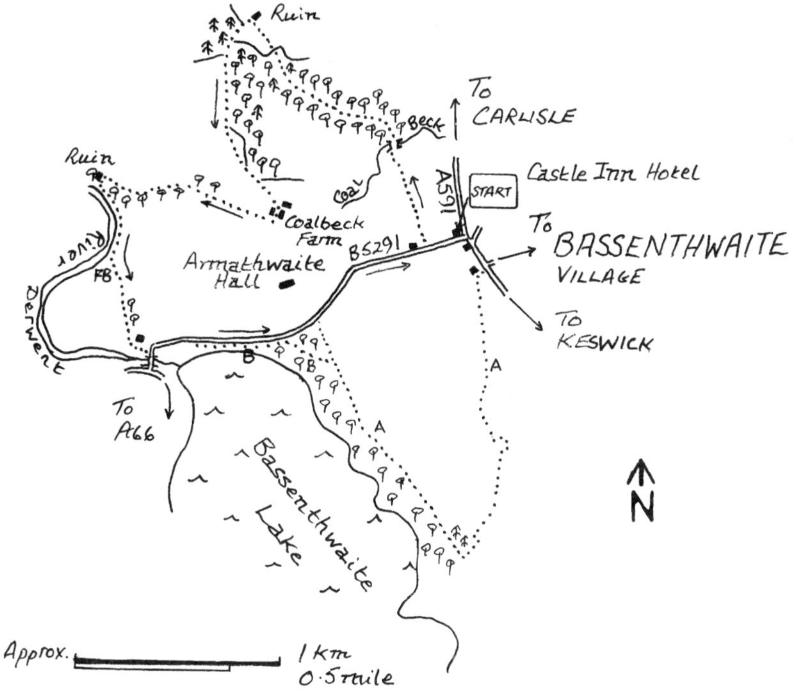

spruce plantation on your right. Go straight over the cross-track on the footpath for Coalbeck Farm and follow the track along the boundary of the wood on your left. The summit dead ahead is Sale Fell. At the next gate leave the track by the stile to the left and cross diagonally over the field to a stile on the far side, dropping down the bank to another track. Turn left to the buildings around Coalbeck Farm. Go to the right in front of the cottages. The development here is associated with the hotel at Armathwaite Hall. Trotters and Friends is a chance to get to know farm animals, including a variety of rare breeds, watch birds, see reptiles and marvel at birds of prey; there is also a riding centre.

Continue by walking right from the entrance and shop and turn to the right by the estate wall (on which you will surely see peacocks) on the bridleway for Isel. You are now on the old road of Buckholme Lonning, which runs between the pens of Trotters and Friends and the wall. Go over a low brow and come to fields on the right. The Lonning swings gradually right and, as it gets close to the river bank, you will find the ruin of a stone hut on the left. Turn left here on the footpath (there is no sign and you need to take care to distinguish this wall gap from others made by all terrain vehicles – a good additional indicator is the summit of Binsey, at right angles, across the fields on the right). Walk through the wood by the river Derwent and keep on the river bank to a footbridge and stile into a field (beside them are the remains of an old iron up and over stile). Climb the low bank and bear right a little towards the pines, keeping along the nearside boundary to a stile with the wood to your left. Continue, to pass the buildings of Herdwick Croft and go half-left round the end of the iron fence to the gate to the road by the two-arched Ouse Bridge. Go left, past the entrance to the caravan site, and continue along the road – looking out for traffic – to return direct to the hotel.

A worthwhile alternative, when the lake level is not too high and the weather has been reasonably good, is to use the routes marked 'A' and 'B' on the sketch map. The National Park Authority owns the bed of the lake and it is a National Nature Reserve. Since the water goes up and down, an informal path has developed along the shore itself, beside the road, amongst the alders and willows. Use this (marked 'B' on the sketch map) and enjoy the views through the trees across the lake. Eventually, swing round the lake end to join a track coming in from the left. (This links to the grounds of Armathwaite Hall by a public path and also has a right fork which is part of the Allerdale Ramble and reaches the road 200 yards short of the lodge. A walk up these will enable you to look at the outside of the Victorian hall. The road was actually lowered so folk like us would not spoil the view! Return.) Follow round the lake end and look immediately for a small stile over the fence on the left into a field. Go over and follow the right-hand boundary and the woodland edge – the area closer to the lake is private.

As you go, you will find there are excellent views of the western slopes of Skiddaw and its associated tops, especially in afternoon sun. Pass a spring and trough by the wood edge and eventually enter woodland of Scots pine. The ground begins to get wet and duck-boards have been laid down. These can be slippery after rain. On the far side of the wood, turn hard left along the boundary (there is no sign) and through a very boggy area which needs care. At the corner of the wood, cross to the left of the fence and continue ahead to a stile. Bassenfell Manor stands out on the low ridge ahead. Towards the far end of this field there is a gate to the right, beside which is a stile with a yellow and white thumb post. Cross over and swing back round the little carr of alders to two more stiles, then bear to the right (a most odd diversion this!). Pass the wooden fence and look for the stile to the right before the oak trees. Cross to the end of the hedge by the telephone poles and continue on the same line to walk up the hedge line to Kiln Hill. A stile gives access to the small caravan site. Take the gate out of this to the yard and walk straight through to the road. Turn left along the verge to return to the hotel.

11 Braithwaite
The Royal Oak

The houses of Braithwaite village lie just off the A66 around the Coledale beck on the western side of the entrance of the Newlands valley. It's a bit of an up-and-downy place and gives little indication of the broad clearing in the forest which its name signifies. The Royal Oak stands tall at the junction of the valley lane with the B5292, which crosses westwards, via the Whinlatter Pass and Thornthwaite Forest, to the Vale of Lorton. Internally, the pub has been pleasantly refurbished at some point and welcomes local and passer-by alike.

In the winter, food is served from 12 noon to 2 pm and 6 pm to 9 pm; summer service is all day. Grilled steaks and gammon seem to be particular favourites but those with smaller appetites can choose various sandwiches and filled jacket potatoes. Notice of vegetarian dishes and of the choice of sweets is posted daily. There is a separate children's menu.

This is a Jennings pub and serves their Bitter, Cocker Hoop and Cumberland Ale. Stout is Guinness, and both Dry Blackthorn and the sweet Taunton Autumn Gold ciders are available. The bar is open from 11 am to 11 pm. A few tables enable you to sit outside on sunny days. There is a family area and games room.

Telephone: 017687 78533.

How to get there: Turn off the A66 about 2 miles west of Keswick. The village is barely a quarter of a mile off the main road.

Parking: Some parking is available at the pub but you should check at the bar before leaving your car while you walk. In addition, there is a little roadside parking in the village.

Length of the walk: 3¾ miles. Map: OS Landranger 90 Penrith, Keswick and Ambleside (pub GR 231236).

The route starts by rounding the shoulder of Barrow and leads up the Newlands valley to Stair. Views across and up the valley are excellent indeed. Return is along the side of the Newlands beck and up the Coledale beck to reach the village. The views over to Skiddaw will be familiar from so many books and postcards.

The Walk

From the main door of the pub, which, because of the steep brow, is on the first floor level, turn sharply round to the left and drop down the narrow street to Low Bridge. Cross the Coledale beck towards the post office and general stores. The village's permanent population is these days only a fraction of what it was in the late 19th century for the mines of Coledale and Newlands are now closed. Walk up the track half-right and go through to meet a lane in 50 yards. Turn up to the left and climb a little to the pink-painted cottages on the right. There is a good view to the east from this point – Latrigg lies beside Keswick town and you can see through the gap towards Penrith, with the isolated cone of Great Mell Fell to the right. Across the road is a small, grassy parking area. Take the path down to the beck from this (there is no sign) and cross over the water and a track into the valley woodland, going sharply up the bank into the field. Continue the same line to a stile and follow along what can be an iris-filled ditch to the farm at Braithwaite Lodge. There is an open view down the valley in which Bassenthwaite Lake lies – you can just see it – and the reedy marshes at the head of the lake are very clear below.

At the sign behind the farm, turn right on the bridleway and walk up the field to a small gate onto the open fell. To the right is the Sleet How ridge of Grisedale Pike. Bear up to the left above the plantation and, on the brow, take a final look back towards Bassenthwaite Lake and Thornthwaite Forest. The track works gently round the shoulder into the main Newlands valley (so named because it was enclosed relatively late, in the late 1200s) and drops steadily down to join the road. Across the far side is the familiar outline of Cat Bells, complemented on your own side of the valley by Rowling End. Walk to the right on the unfenced road. I once surprised a redstart amongst the gorse on the lower slopes here. A little

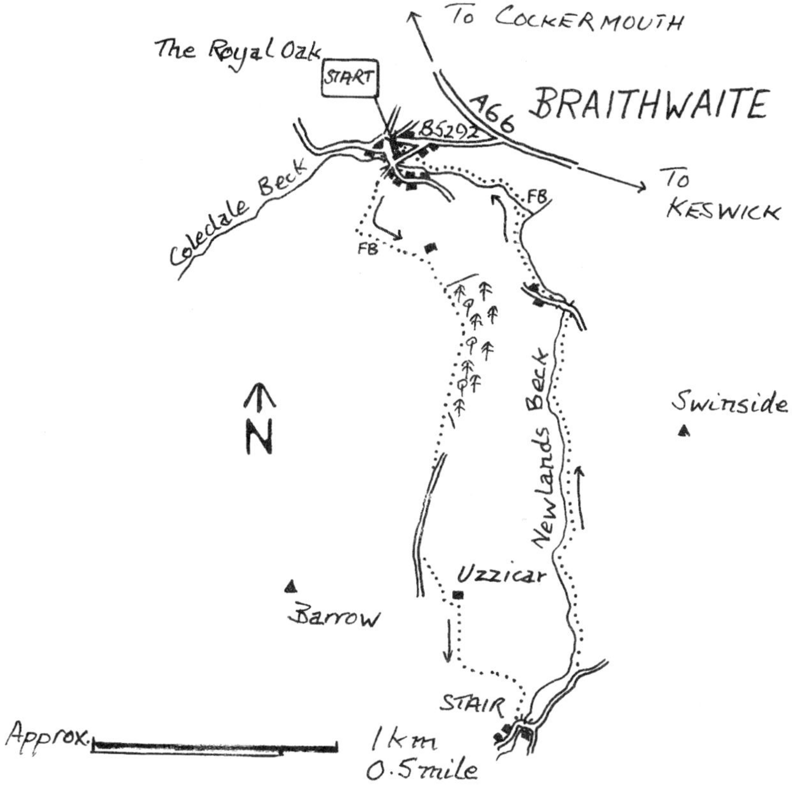

way along you pass a fine example of a landslip of the unstable material from which Barrow is made. Just beyond this, go left on the track for Uzzicar and follow through, right of the farm gate and trees, across the old spoil heaps of a mine, to find a stile over the fence. The Stair Hotel is visible across to your right.

Follow the old hedge line on the left and go straight ahead at the next stile. Do not go to the right through the gate but keep ahead and swing right to the telegraph pole to pick up the track upstream. It is sheltered in the valley bottom and, in summer, warblers frequent the streamside trees and red admirals flutter across the field in the sun. It is hardly believable that German miners smelted copper here in the days of the first Elizabeth. The Goldscope mine (the English version of Gottesgab, which means God's gift), just up the valley, was extremely rich.

Walk through the field gate and turn to the left over the stone bridge to pass in front of the Adventure Centre in the hamlet of Stair. Follow the lane marked for Portinscale as far as the footpath to the left beyond the sports field. Dead ahead are the forested slopes of Swinside. Walk down the beck now beneath trees and with a view of Dodd, below Skiddaw, in front of you. Continue past the stone bridge (which leads back to Uzzicar) and use the path along the flood bank, covered in harebells, knapweed and ragwort in the summer months. Behind is a deceptive view of High Crags, which appears to end the valley but, in fact, it dog-legs to continue beyond. Coleridge could see this view from his window in Keswick and vividly records in his diary the changes of the scene in sun and rain. At the lane, go left over the bridge.

Bear almost immediately right between the house and barn at Lower Braithwaite and continue downstream on the opposite bank. Cross the footbridge over the Coledale beck by the ford and walk left upstream beside the campsite through to the village. Cross over the road and use the unmade lane to return to the rear of the Royal Oak.

A short distance up the Whinlatter road is what is probably the finest forest visitor centre in the North of England, which is well worth a diversion to visit.

12 Rosthwaite
The Scafell Hotel

Rosthwaite village crowds closely around the narrow road through the valley. 'Thwaite' means a clearing in old Norse, but whether it was a rushy one or a stony one seems unclear – either would fit perfectly well. In 1772, Rev William Gilpin thought this an idyllic, pastoral spot. The Scafell Hotel is at the southern end of the village, between the road and the Stonethwaite beck. It has been an inn for, perhaps, 170 years but before that was the vicarage for a short while and, even earlier, the home for the mine manager of the wad mines (wad is the local name for the form of carbon known as graphite, plumbago, or pencil lead, which explains why pencils are still made in Keswick; the mine was higher up the valley, in Newhouse Gill, above Seatoller). It is an imposing building for its location and is surrounded by fine gardens. The bar, where walkers are very welcome, occupies the rear of this country hotel and its windows overhang the beck.

Meals are available from 12 noon to 2 pm (snacks are served until 5 pm) and 6.30 pm to 9 pm. Smoked Seathwaite trout (Seathwaite is the next hamlet up the valley) would be a grand starter for home-made lasagne or local gammon. Omelettes, salads, a delicious game pie, hot and cold sandwiches and filled jacket potatoes extend your range of choice greatly, and vegetarians are well catered for too. Children's portions are available and there is a family area. Afternoon teas are served and include Cumberland rum butter.

The hotel is a freehouse. Theakston BB, XB, Old Peculier and Mild are on draught with Jennings Cockermouth ales and guest beers. Stouts are Guinness and Murphy's, lagers Carlsberg, Beck's, and Coors and ciders are both Strongbow and Woodpecker. Part of the gardens make a fine area in which to sit out and admire the scenery. Please ask before taking your dog inside.

Telephone: 017687 77208.

How to get there: Use the B5289, either from Keswick or over the Honister Pass from Buttermere.

Parking: At the hotel, but please notify reception if you want to leave your car while you walk. There are also two public parking areas close to the village hall.

Length of the walk: 3¼ miles. Map: OS Landranger 90 Penrith, Keswick and Ambleside (hotel GR 259148).

Upper Borrowdale (without a lake) is, perhaps, the very essence of mountain Lakeland, being hemmed in so closely by high tops. The route of this walk captures that feeling, with only a couple of short, steeper sections of the fellside. The circuit includes famous Johnny Wood, Castle Crag and a fine view down Derwentwater.

The Walk

Cross the road outside the hotel and use the footpath along the lane behind the cottages, keeping to the left at Nook Farm, where the yew tree overhangs the wall. Turn to the right before Stonecroft onto the footpath for Longthwaite. Follow the clear path through the fields, bearing half-right at the stile and go through the gate to join a lane beside Peat House. The snub end of Buck How, ahead, divides Langstrath, to the left, from Seathwaite and Grains Gill, to the right – both are approaches to the highest point in England at Scafell Pike (3,206 ft).

Go to the right, along a lane with huge boulders in the wall on the left – which is an indication of some considerable age – and cross the bridge over the river Derwent. Immediately to the left is the entrance to Longthwaite Youth Hostel. Go through the gateway and turn right up the wall of the farm buildings (there is no sign), entering Johnny Wood through the kissing-gate at the corner of the field. This National Trust property is a famous place for non-flowering plants, to be found amongst the rocks on the ground and on the bark of the old trees. Its management is carefully

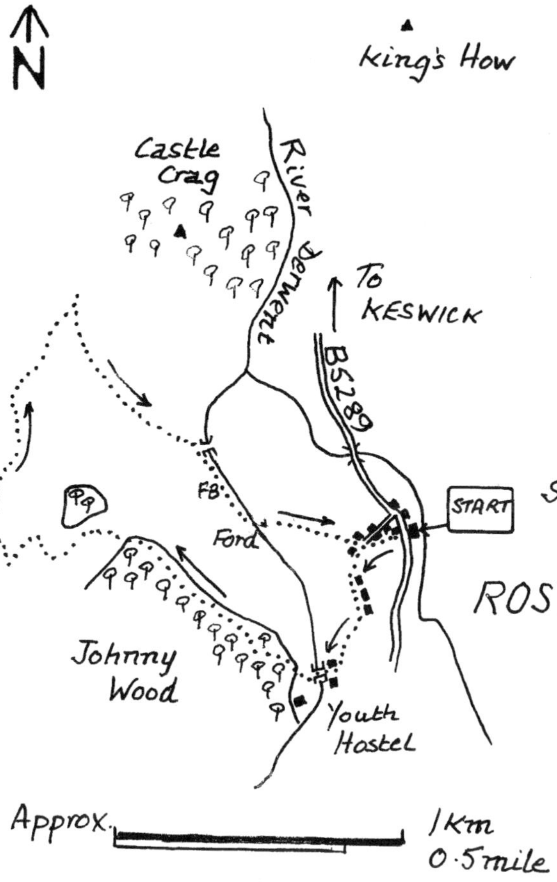

controlled and sheep are allowed to graze in order to keep ground vegetation down. The stony, but easy, path wanders along the bottom of the wood. In many places along the field walls to the right are examples of pollarded ash trees, which are still cut above the reach of grazing beasts.

At the far end of the wood, follow the track up the fellside to the left, more or less parallel to Scaleclose Gill, ignoring the path down and across the gill, which leads to Scaleclose Coppice on the far bank. Go up towards the crags of High Scawdel and take no notice of the up and over stile on the left. Cross the farm bridge over the gill and climb gently, then steeply, up the field to a small gate at the fell wall in the top right-hand corner. Turn right along the bridleway (part of the Allerdale Ramble). Castle Crag is immediately before you with King's How – the other half of the 'Jaws of Borrowdale' – across to its right. Skiddaw is visible through the gap to the left. (Down, close to the road, right in the Jaws is the Bowder Stone – a 1,900 ton block, balanced almost on a knife edge.) The path contours the slope, with a fine view to the right, across the ridge between High Seat and Ullscarf, towards Helvellyn; the path from Watendlath (which features in several of Hugh Walpole's *Rogue Herries* novels) is clear between Brund Fell and Yew Crag. At the hause between Castle Crag and Lobstone Band, continue ahead for 100 yards to the memorial to the Rescue Dog 'Honey'. There is a magnificent view down Derwentwater to Keswick, Skiddaw and Blencathra from this point.

Retrace your steps to the footpath over the wall to the left at the junction of the walls. Swing round the shoulder to a wide view up the valley, with Glaramara and Great Gable up to the right. (For a better view, both up and down the valley, work your way up left to the gate and go steeply up to the top of the Crag. This was one of Father West's 'stations' for viewing Derwentwater, noted in his *Guide* of 1778.) The grass of these slopes is rich in orchids, harebells and hawkweeds in summer, but can be slippery underfoot when wet. Drop down rapidly to the fields beside the river, past a row of fine old oaks. Ignore the river bridge and stay on the same side over the footbridge beside the larch trees. Walk upstream in the shade of alders, ash and sycamore on the built-up flood bank until you reach the stepping stones at the ford. Cross left and bear right on the track towards the village. Go left at Yew Tree Farm and pass the village hall to the junction of the road opposite the shop. Turn right, through the narrow section, by the Royal Oak – where Wordsworth probably stayed in 1812 – to return to the start.

13 Threlkeld
The Salutation Inn

Threlkeld village lies at the base of the slopes of the mountain usually referred to today by its old Celtic name of Blencathra, though the Victorians called it Saddleback – from its distinctive shape when seen from a distance. Sometime, 800 to 900 years ago, a group of serfs (or thralls) put down roots by one of the springs issuing from the fell side and gave the settlement its name. Mines and quarries made it a more active place in the 19th century but it has sunk back into quietness again. The Salutation (the name of the pub is derived from the huntsman's greeting) is by the main street at the eastern end of the village. The building is early 1700s and its beams are, reputedly, old ships' timbers. Its link with the hunt continues and there is still a social here in January each year.

Food is available from 12 noon to 2 pm and 6.30 pm (7 pm on Sundays) to 9 pm. The steak and mushroom pie is extremely popular, but there is also a considerable choice of internationally inspired dishes. Basket meals, salads and sandwiches cater for the less hungry. No doubt the children will be tempted by a 'Big Sally' – an affectionate reference to the pub name – the local variant on the burger. Choice is extended at the height of the summer season.

As a Scottish and Newcastle house, Theakston BB and Old Peculier are served, and a couple of guest beers. Stouts are Guinness and Gillespies, the lager is McEwan's and the ciders Strongbow and Woodpecker. Winter opening hours for the bar are 12 noon to 2 pm and 6 pm to 11 pm (7 pm to 10.30 pm on Sundays). In the summer it opens at 11 am, closes at 3 pm and opens again at 5 30 pm. You will find a beer garden, a small garden area for the children, and a section for families upstairs. Well-behaved dogs are welcomed. Linked self-catering accommodation is available for a longer stay.

Telephone: 017687 79614.

How to get there: Follow either sign from the main A66, between Keswick and Penrith, into the village and go up the main street to the inn.

Parking: At the pub, but please check at the bar before leaving your car while you walk. There is also a National Park car park a little further up Blease Road from the footpath turn.

Length of the walk: 5 miles. Map: OS Landranger 90 Penrith, Keswick and Ambleside (inn GR 323254).

The route links the interest of the village with wide views to the south and the woodlands and gorge of the river Greta. The return is along the bed of the old railway line. No lengthy ascents are involved.

The Walk

Leave the pub door to the left and walk along the village street to the church of St Mary on the left, just past the other village pub, the Horse and Farrier. A priest was recorded at Threlkeld as early as 1220 but the building you see is of 1777, though the bells are older. Inside, the font is of granite from the quarry across the valley. There is a fine view of Blencathra between the churchyard trees, that is especially pleasing in the spring when the daffodils are in bloom. Continue along the street and turn up to the right along Blease Road, past the Mission Room of 1885. The road goes moderately steeply up for a short way. Turn left on the footpath by Town Head and pass the cottages, into the field. Over your right shoulder is a view up Blease Gill towards the mountain summit.

As you continue awhile the view to the left (to the south) is wide and stretches from the quarries, below Threlkeld Knotts, through the Vale of St John towards Helvellyn, over High Rigg and the Naddle valley, to Cat Bells, beyond Derwentwater, and the wide sweep of fells to the south-west. At the far side of the field take the left-hand gate and go ahead to a kissing-gate, followed by a stone stile and an up and over stile, through the narrowing of the field and below the barn. Go between the big oaks, bearing up slightly to the stone stile right of the bottom tree by the far

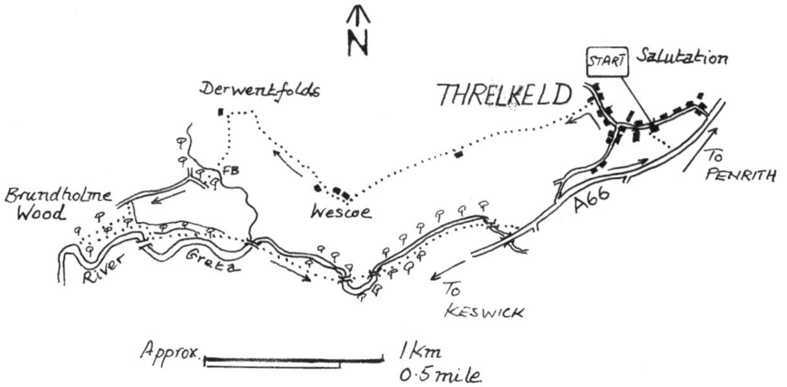

wall. A more obvious path leads right of the house at Ings and a notice for a diversion indicates you should follow the arrow at the up and over stile. Up to your right now is the old isolation hospital, which has become a Field Centre. Take the direct route through, past the oak with the white paint flash, leaving the cottage to the left, and reach the lane at Wescoe. The stone circle on Castle Rigg is clearly visible across the valley, directly above the barn on the crest between the trees.

Bear round to the right on the lane through this tiny farm hamlet. One of the houses here has an imposing triangular pediment over the door. Walk up the lane into the Glenderaterra valley, with roses and pollarded ash in the hedgerows. The spire of St Mary's church in Keswick should be clear down the valley to your left and the bulk of Lonscale Fell rises, half-left, obscuring Skiddaw from sight. Follow the lane round the bend to the buildings of Derwentfolds and turn left, just before them, on the footpath along the old track towards Keswick. Drop down beside a small beck lined with big oak trees and cross the footbridge beside the old ford in the woods at the bottom. Climb the bends of the track through the wood and, at the junction with the lane, turn right, go up 200 yards to a triangle junction and bear to the left. The road now contours along the valley side and drops gently down to meet the corner of Brundholme Wood in about 400 yards.

Immediately go left down the fence line on a permissive path for 20 yards to meet a track and walk down it to the right amongst old coppices of hazel with standard oak trees scattered through them. After about 400 yards a path crosses over the track and you can turn left along this to drop down to the main path beside the tumbling river Greta. (Should you miss out on the left turn, the track continues down and still meets the same riverside path.) Go left, upstream, and exit the wood to a field, dropping down the bank to the right (it is often wet just here) before crossing over to the bed of the old railway by the bridge. Turn left and follow the track to the main road.

The railway linked Cockermouth and Penrith from 1862 to 1970. As you walk along you will pass two shelters. The first contains information about the views, farming and the life in the river; the second has information about the railway itself. Beside the track you will find a great variety of wildflowers and some interesting mosses and liverworts growing on the damp rocks of the cutting. At the next bridge is the junction of the Glenderaterra and the Glenderamackin, which flow from the two sides of Blencathra and form the Greta here.

Just before the main road bridge a footbridge leads left for the path up to the roadside. Beneath the new road bridge is the old one. Go up to the A66 and walk along the verge to the second footpath to the left, which returns you to the start.

14 Thirlspot
The King's Head Hotel

Thirlmere – a reservoir as we see it today – lies between the ridge of Helvellyn, to the east, and the lower High Seat and Armboth fells on the west. Such village as there ever was used to be at Wythburn, at the head of the valley, and Thirlspot (the Giant's Pool) is just the hotel and a farm. Most folk drive through, a few stop for a drink and a something to eat at the hotel or in one of the car parks; not many take much of a walk in the valley itself – which is a great pity. There has been a hostelry here for many a long year and the view of the long, low-seeming building from the front, with Brown Crag behind, is the essence of Lakeland. Whatever the weather you will find a good welcome.

The menu at the King's Head is very extensive indeed and it is hard to convey more than a flavour of the choices available to you. It is also unusual in that it gives a careful indication of the availability of half-portions for children and of dishes suitable for vegetarians (in addition to their special menus). Betraying my own origins, I went for a local trout pâté followed by Lancashire hotpot, and the stomach-clinging joy of jam roly-poly – which all went well with the crisp winter sunshine of the day. You could, equally easily, be wholly international in your selection. Salads, sandwiches and ploughman's lunches are also on offer. Serving times are from 12 noon to 3 pm and 6 pm to 9.30 pm (all day in the summer).

Beers, in this freehouse, are Theakston BB, Old Peculier and Mild and a guest ale. Stouts are Guinness and Murphy's, the lager is McEwan's and there is cider on draught. Wines are also available by the glass. There is a no-smoking area inside, in addition to the restaurant. The beer garden, in front of the hotel, is large and has superb views. Families are most welcome and there is a play area for the children. Dogs are permitted in the bar, which is open from 11 am to 11 pm on Monday to Saturday, and 12 noon to 3 pm and 7 pm to 10.30 pm on Sundays. Accommodation is available.

Telephone: 017687 72393.

How to get there: The hotel stands beside the main A591 between Keswick and Ambleside. Regular bus services pass the door.

Parking: At the hotel. There is also parking to the south at Swirls car park, at Station Coppice car park, across the road, and to the north at Legburthwaite car park (entrance off the B5322, the St John's in the Vale to Threlkeld road).

Length of the walk: 5½ miles. Inclusion of the Swirls nature trail would add about another 2 miles. Map: OS Landranger 90 Penrith, Keswick and Ambleside (hotel GR 317177).

The valley in which Thirlmere lies is surprisingly pleasant and the circuit along the lower fellside and through the woods on the shore is most enjoyable. Views to the ridges on either side, and to the north, are excellent. The path is by no means flat and even, but there is little climbing involved. The area has an interesting literary heritage.

The Walk

Start by going to the left along the building from the front door and left again into the farmyard at the end. Cross straight up the yard to the field gate and walk up to the bridge over the large open leet. Continue up the wall on the left to the fell wall and join the contour path going south, up the valley. Go over the small beck. There is a good view to the western side of the valley as far as Launchy Gill, which drops steeply down through the forest (there is a nature trail here, accessible from the western shore road). Work your way round the small cliffs and the scree of Brown How. The path is stony and partly built up. Eventually you drop beside a wall to a footbridge. Continue beyond for about 400 yards to the corner of the plantations and go down right and cross another footbridge into Swirls car park. (An addition to the route would be to include the circular Swirls nature trail from this car park – this requires an extra hour or so.)

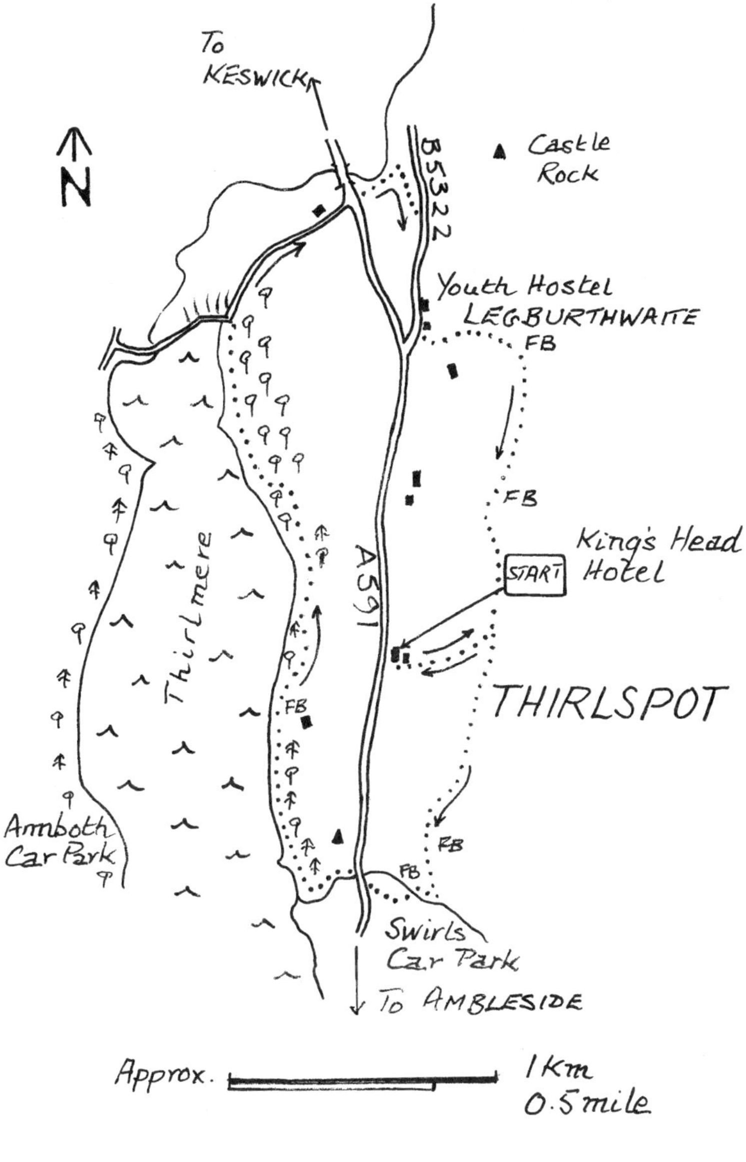
To KESWICK
N
B5322
Castle Rock
Youth Hostel
LEGBURTHWAITE
FB
FB
King's Head Hotel
START
THIRLSPOT
A591
Thirlmere
FB
FB
FB
Armboth Car Park
Swirls Car Park
To AMBLESIDE
Approx.
1Km
0.5 mile

Cross over the main road with great care and walk along the verge to the Station Coppice car park, 50 yards down. Make the minor diversion through the small gate in the back wall and climb up the rocky knoll behind. This explains the reason for the name – which is nothing to do with railways or buses – but arises from the fact that this was one of Father West's 'stations' for fine views in his *Guide* of 1778. It is still a fine view, which extends right round – in addition to the enclosing ridges, the Skiddaw–Blencathra massif is visible to the north. The view, however, has changed significantly. What he saw were two smaller lakes at a lower level, linked by narrows at Armboth, to your left a little, and crossed by causeways and bridges – what he didn't see were the extensive coniferous plantations, which are all post-1908.

Return to the gate and take the path down the field, towards the lake, beside the Helvellyn beck. A kissing-gate gives access to the plantations of larch and spruce. Drop down to the shore and bear right along the permissive path through the woods. At all seasons these are a delight, being cool in summer, a riot of colour in the autumn, crisp with snow in winter and a flush of delicate green of the larches in spring. There is something of a gap in the tree canopy behind the large hotel at Dalehead, where there are two footbridges. Go up to the right a little and pass along the field edge by a water trough. At the kissing-gate go up to the right and over the rocky bluff to join a path which contours round Great How through oak woods. (The path left goes to the shore and is difficult, even when the water is low enough to get round the bluff.) Eventually, steps descend onto the lane which crosses the dam (there is no sign here).

It is worth the diversion left to the plaque which records the opening of the reservoir in 1894. This is a fine example of civic pride and superbly presented in red sandstone, as is the castellated works entrance in the wood. The water originally flowed 96 miles to the Manchester area entirely by gravity, whereas these days it is interrupted by the treatment works at Watchgate, near Kendal. The whole catchment of 10,000 acres was bought by the city of Manchester and about 2,000 acres were planted. Return to the steps and continue along the lane, passing cottages on the left hung with green slate to keep out the weather, then walk to the main road beyond High Bridgend Farm and its campsite. (Here, in about 1816, de Quincey recorded coming upon the farmer one night mooning himself, as others would sun themselves!)

Go straight over the A591 with great care and through the gate onto the old lane, right of the St John's beck bridge and with sycamores on the left. Immediately in front is Castle Rock of Triermain, often with climbers visible. Its name derives from the fancy that the jagged outline of its top looks like the battlements of a castle. The Triermain part was added by the Victorians after Sir Walter Scott was inspired by his visits here, in the company of Wordsworth, to write a popular poem *The Bridal of*

Triermain, in 1805. Walk until level with a picnic site to the left and go right through the small gate into Legburthwaite car park. Cross through and exit onto the narrow B5322. Walk, with care, past the tiny mission building (1881) and the lap-boarded Youth Hostel to the footpath to the left by the telephone box.

Go up the lane by the cottages and farm and take the up and over stile signed for Sticks Pass. About 10 yards up, turn right on the permissive path for Swirls car park and climb up a little further to the corner of the fell wall. The path wanders along the contour, passing behind Fisher Place farm – where painter and poet Dante Gabriel Rosetti spent the last holiday of his life in 1881. From this point there is a good view of the sheep shearing in July. Go over Fisher Gill, cross a footbridge and continue to the junction with the path up from Thirlspot. Return down to the hotel.

15 Dacre
The Horse and Farrier

The Dacre beck joins the river Eamont south-west of Penrith and its valley marks the change from the Lakeland fells to the richer agricultural lands of Cumbria. It is no surprise that this spot was chosen as the site of a monastery and then as the stronghold for the area. The pub stands up the bank a little from the village proper and looks out over the valley of the 'trickling brook' which gave its name to the owners of the castle and the settlement itself. It is a plainly attractive building, of about 1750 and in farmhouse style, with its yard open to the road on one side and the old barn complementing the house directly across from it, with the pub created out of an adjacent cottage. Inside it is cosy and snug and has escaped modernisation.

Food is served from 12 noon to 2 pm and 6 pm to 9 pm (though it is not available on winter weekdays from New Year until March). Sandwiches, salads, snacks and toasties are complemented by a main menu and a specials board (including vegetarian meals). Steak and kidney, mixed grills and Cumberland sausage are especially popular. There is a children's menu and a take-away service is also on offer.

At this freehouse, the bar is open from 12 noon to 3 pm and 6 pm to 11 pm on weekdays and Saturdays – the hours may be extended a little in the middle of the day in summer – and on Sundays the times are 7 pm to 10.30 pm in the evening. Worthington BB and Bass bitter and mild are on draught and there is a guest beer, which is changed weekly. The lager is Carling and cider is Dry Blackthorn. There is space for a few tables outside. Dogs are not permitted inside.

Telephone: 017684 86541.

How to get there: Approach, following signs to the village, from the A592 or the A66 west of Penrith.

Parking: There is only limited parking opposite and in front of the pub, so please ask at the bar before leaving your car while you walk. Additional roadside parking is possible in the village.

Length of the walk: 4 miles. Map: OS Landranger 90 Penrith, Keswick and Ambleside (pub GR 458266).

Dacre village possesses one of the most interesting churches in Cumbria (which I suggest you look at last) and the unique tower of the castle. Down the richly farmed valley is Dalemain, a fascinating house with much to see, close to the old county boundary at the river Eamont. The return is via the woodlands of the valley side, with views into the higher fells. Most of the route is easy walking.

The Walk

Walk down the hill from the pub yard and turn to the left, between the house and barn, at the fork of the roads, onto the track which swings towards the castle. This is a single, large, defensive tower with a moat. It is now a private home and not open to viewing – despite this, it is fairly easy to see its main features. Built in the early 14th century by Lord Dacre, the existing larger windows were added in about 1700 and, shortly afterwards, it came into the hands of the Hasells of Dalemain. Continue along the track past the barns and drop down the bank, past the little plantation, and towards the Dacre beck. Ahead is a fine view to the highest point of the Pennines, Cross Fell, and of Dun Fell, marked out by its radio station. This is good pasture land mixed with some arable and plantations and woods. The red soil of the track side is rich, in their season, with speedwells, vetches, red campion, stitchwort, buttercups and cow parsley and I have watched awhile a redstart flicking in and out of a small copse of alders. The track is lined with a young avenue of planted oak, elm and poplar.

Rise a little as you reach the bend of the beck and walk beside a high wall on the right, covered in rue, to the car park for Dalemain with its adjacent picnic site. The house and gardens are open daily between April

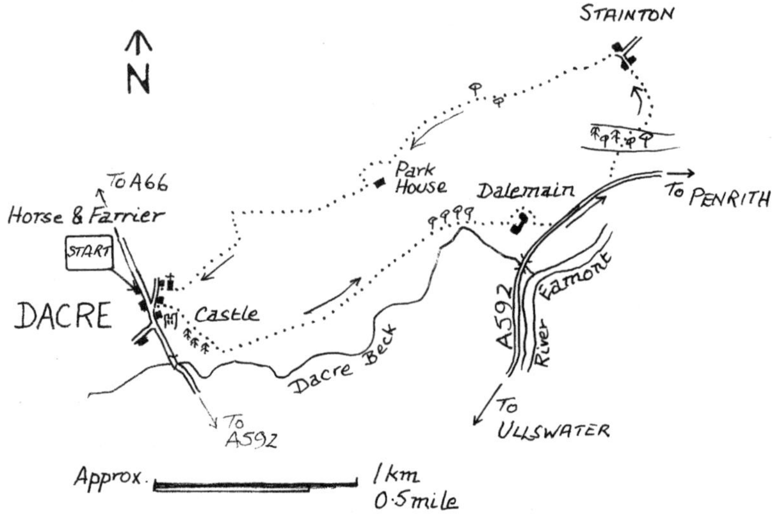

and October, and tickets are sold at the gate. The façade is mid-1700s but the internal core is Elizabethan and there is much of interest. Included are museums of the Westmorland and Cumberland Yeomanry, a countryside museum, a collection of old agricultural machinery and a fell pony museum. The gardens have a collection of old-style roses and a massive Greek fir.

Leave down the driveway to the main road and walk along to the left for about a quarter of a mile to a footpath to the left, more or less opposite the house on the bank of the river Eamont, which formed the old boundary between Cumberland and Westmorland. Go up the field to the stile in the right-hand corner and into Evening Bank Wood, edged with beech and sycamore. The view back at the wood edge is of Dunmallard Hill, above Pooley Bridge at the bottom of Ullswater, and across the lake towards Martindale and Place Fell. Climb up through the mixed woodland, on a slightly muddy path, to some steps up a small cliff which lead to a stile into a field at the top. Turn immediately right and left over the stone stile, with a view over to the town of Penrith, and cross to the ruin of a barn. Use the gate between the walls and go past an orchard on your left to walk between the pink and white houses. Turn left and right through the gate and enter the top of Stainton village.

Bear round to the left, by Torr House, on the track marked for Dacre, between the garage and the bungalow. At the fork, continue straight on between limestone walls covered in ivy and herb robert and under overhanging branches as you reach the top of the rise. A stile leads into the field. Go right into the wood and use the up and over stile to a gate. You can now see the upper Ullswater valley and Dalemain lies down on your left. Bear right to a stile in the fence and drop half-left to the end of the wall in the bottom, crossing through the narrow belt of trees. Follow the left-hand boundary to an up and over stile by a copse of conifers and follow the arrow ahead to a gate, hidden by the wall, on the far side of the field. Turn left towards the buildings of Park House and follow the arrows round and along the topside of the wall. Stay with the farm track to an up and over stile sited below the tall barn, up on the bank to your right. Walk slowly round and up the brow to a stile in the fence and ahead to another up and over stile. You may see wheatears flitting in and out of the wall along this section as you admire the view of the castle and church below. Ahead is the cone of Little Mell Fell. Follow the old green track down the bank to enter the churchyard by the green gate on the right.

Immediately to your right are two of the famous stone bears of Dacre, which probably mark the four corners of the original graveyard. No one knows their real age, though they seem to be medieval. They tell something of a story if taken in the order north-west, south-west, south-east, north-east – you will find details inside the church. St Andrew's (it was once on Scottish land after all) is Norman and is probably on the site of the former Saxon monastery recorded by Bede in AD 698 (re-used Roman stones have been found). Inside there are fragments of cross shafts and a chained Bible. Somewhere close by Kings Athelstan (of Northumbria), Constantine (of Scots), Owain (of South Wales and father of the Dunmail who was killed on the Raise of that name), Hywel (of West Wales) and Ealdulf (of Bernicia – which ran from the Tees to the Forth) met and made peace in AD 926. Leave the main church gate and go left and right to return to the pub.

16 Allonby
The Ship Hotel

The coast of the English side of the Solway Firth is very distinctive and it is designated as an Area of Outstanding Natural Beauty. The industrial area of West Cumberland, such as it is, ends at Maryport and the low, gentle curve of Allonby Bay extends from Sea Brows, at the northern end of Maryport, for about 7 miles to Dubmill Point. The village straggles along the shore and is cut in two by Allonby beck. A few yards to the north of the bridge is the Ship Hotel. The beach was an attraction as early as the mid-1700s and, though the Ship is not dated, we know it was in existence a century later when Charles Dickens and Wilkie Collins stayed there in 1857 (Collins sprained his ankle and so the visit was longer than planned). Its tall frontage still faces the buffeting gales and its high-ceilinged bar and restaurant (with Dickens prints) are still welcoming.

Food is available daily from 12 noon to 2 pm and 7 pm to 9 pm. The selection caters for all tastes, including vegetarians and children. In keeping with the great author, game pie might be a suitable choice! Specialist dinner menus are offered and, as these change with some frequency, it is wise to check by phone first.

The bar is open from 11 am to 3 pm and 7 pm to 11 pm (10.30 on Sundays). Yates ales are served here, brewed in nearby Westnewton –

Premium and Bitter. Additonally, there is Younger Scotch ale alongside a different guest beer each week. Dry Blackthorn cider, Stella Artois and McEwan's lagers and Guinness are on draught. The dining room is non-smoking and there is a games area suitable for families. A public play area for children lies directly across the beck. Dogs are not permitted during food service hours.

Telephone: 01900 881017.

How to get there: The hotel is on the B5300 between Maryport and Silloth. An alternative approach would be cross-country, from the A596 at Aspatria, on the B5301, turning left in Westnewton.

Parking: There is a limited amount of parking at the hotel and a series of public car parks along the shore.

Length of the walk: 5½ miles. Except for the furthest section between Blue Dial Farm and Crosscanonby, the walk can be shortened to any length which suits the occasion. Map: OS Landranger 85 Carlisle (hotel GR 081429).

This walk is highly dependent on the weather and season – at its best on a clear, calm day, of course, but bracing and exciting when the wind comes in from the sea. The difference between the shingle-side walk in the one direction and the inner shore in the other can also be marked. Allonby, itself, is a mini-resort and Crosscanonby an ancient settlement.

The Walk

Cross straight over the road from the doorway and go a few paces right to the footbridge over the beck. This is channelled now but Sir George Head recorded stepping stones in 1836, and photographs on the wall of the Corner Shop (by the bridge) show horses being taken to water much later than that. Turn right and then left, beside the large square building called The Hill, once a brewery and now stables, and walk through the playground onto the edge of the shore. If the weather is calm, and the sea is out, you can turn left along the shingle shore itself; otherwise, take the path which wanders along the edge of the grassy area through patches of marram and a scattering of flowers.

The whole length of the shore is extremely popular with West Cumbrian and Carlisle families at summer weekends. At bank holidays it can be hard to fit the proverbial 'pin between them'! The grass areas inshore are cut by the Council and are pounded by many feet – human, dog and pony – so the turf is short and the wildflowers few; there is a series of car parks and picnic benches. Once away from the village, and beyond the first lane inland, growth is lusher and a greater variety of

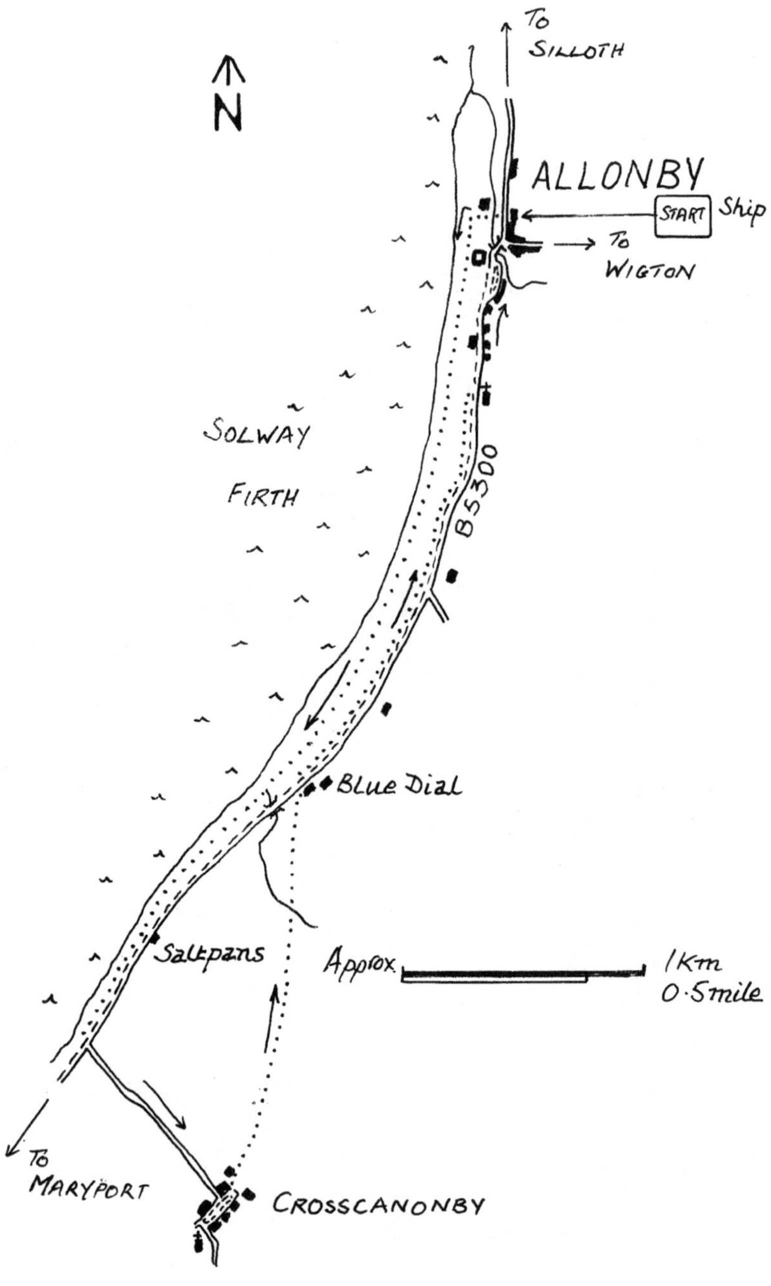
N
To
SILLOTH
ALLONBY
START
Ship
To
WIGTON
SOLWAY
FIRTH
B5300
Blue Dial
Saltpans
Approx.
1Km
0·5mile
To
MARYPORT
CROSSCANONBY

plants survive. Continue along the shingle to the low clay cliff of Swarthy Hill, accompanied by gulls, oystercatchers and curlews. Rough-woven hurdles have been inserted to try to control the sand blowing in the wind.

Just beyond the enclosure of cobbles on the left is a Cumbria Coastal Way fingerpost – this is also part of the Allerdale Ramble. Turn across the road to a small car park beside the excavated foundations of the former salt works, overshadowed by some wind-bent sycamores (there were several information signs at this site but vandals keep destroying them). Salt was made here from medieval times until 1730 and the cottages were lived in until the 19th century. Climb up the steps in the low cliff. From the top enjoy the view southwards to the greater height of Sea Brows, at Maryport, and enter the field to see the outline of the Roman signal station. There is a fine view inland, too, to the fells around Grasmoor, behind Cockermouth. Return back to the shore side of the road.

Continue, amongst thrift and marram, past a section of shore which seems especially attractive to flocks of small waders at high tide. At the next car park, turn left on the lane for Crosscanonby (behind the bracken covered bank are some public toilets). Cross over the marshy area of willow and alder and climb up the brow to the village. Swing round the green to the right and to the church of St John the Evangelist. A Roman altar was found in 1880 and a number of other Roman stones are incorporated in the fabric of the building, so this is certainly an ancient site – the fort of Alauna was at Maryport. The tradition that St Ninian might have been here in the 4th century AD (his base was across the Solway at Whithorn) and St Kentigern (Mungo) in the 6th is believable. Inside the church, the chancel arch is a re-erected Roman arch, put up by John Senhouse, of Netherhall. Outside, in the graveyard, just beyond the door, lies John Smith, salt tax officer, in an elaborately carved red sandstone tomb and, by the south-east end, is a hog back gravestone.

Go back to the top of the green and walk along. Bear down left at the far end, opposite East Farm, and take the track past the bungalow (there is no sign). You drop into a dry valley. At the bend, use the second of the two steel gates to the left and continue the line to a gate in the dyke at the top of the brow. Head for the gate in the left-hand corner of the next field. The path continues on more or less the same line to a stile in the far hedge. Cross again to a further stile, which takes you to the other side of the hedge. Angle right for the gate and go over the field to the bottom corner by the beck. There should be a footbridge here but it was missing when I last passed that way (the farmer kindly suggested I use the field gate and walk down the beck to the farm bridge instead). On the far side of the beck, head for the left-hand end of the buildings of Blue Dial Farm and find a stile to the road (there is no sign). Cross the road and head back towards the village along the roadside.

Return back across the road to the footway at Christ Church (1744, rebuilt in 1845). Inside this strangely severe building is a memorial to a local boy, Joseph Huddart, who, in the mid-1700s, found a new way of making rope cables which evened out the strain on the strands, so reducing the numbers of deaths caused by whip-lashing when cables snapped. Pass the caravan site, a restaurant, and some modern houses. On the opposite verge is an old stone milestone. Though the lettering is very worn I thought I could just make out 'Workington 11' and 'Wigton 12'. A terrace of cottages is set back from the road, some of them low built, as though to huddle for shelter from the winter wind. A shop and hotel come next and then there is a gap to the bridge. On the far side of the beck there is, even today, a hugger-mugger of houses, barns and sheds, which still fits well with the description left by Dickens and Collins in their *Lazy Tour of Two Idle Apprentices*. Cross the bridge to return to the Ship.

17 Abbeytown
The Wheatsheaf Inn

The quiet agricultural scene of the countryside around Abbeytown belies an exciting past. The lands at the head of the Solway Firth were, for many centuries, under the sway of kings from the north (Scotland as it eventually became) and were fully a part of England only after 1157. This low rise, barely 100 ft above sea level, is the holm (the island) from which the abbey took its name. The Wheatsheaf, as a building, manages both to fit in and create a surprise. Standing between the main village junction and the abbey, it could have come from a Kent or Sussex village. In fact, it was built in 1935 as one of the chain of State Managed Brewery houses, a scheme, based in Carlisle, which was intended to control the drinking habits of munitions workers during World War I and was finally wound up in 1971. Inside, the pub is spacious and bright.

Food service is from 12 noon to 2 pm and 6 pm (7 pm on Sundays) to 9 pm (but not on Mondays, except for bank holidays). Serious eaters will find the mixed grill is very substantial indeed, but there are also good fish choices, omelettes, salads, pizzas and burgers. The children's specials include their own version of Cumberland sausage and there are several vegetarian dishes.

A freehouse these days, the bar opens from 11 am to 11 pm (10.30 pm on Sundays), but may have more restricted hours during the winter season. Beers are Tetley Bitter and Mild, stout is Murphy's, lagers both Stella Artois and Carlsberg and the cider is Dry Blackthorn. There is a play area for children as well as a beer garden. A family room is available too. Dogs are not permitted inside the building.

Telephone: 016973 61317.

How to get there: Abbeytown can be reached on the B5302 from the A596 via Wigton, or on the B5307 via Kirkbride from Carlisle.

Parking: There is a large car park at the pub, but please ask at the bar before leaving your car while you walk. A small amount of additional parking exists at the roadside by the abbey.

Length of the walk: 3½ miles. Map: OS Landranger 85 Carlisle (pub GR 474507).

Holme Cultram Abbey is an outstanding remnant of the past importance of this place and its links with Scotland are particularly interesting. This gently undulating walk circuits through agricultural land from the village via the river Waver and has views across the marshes.

The Walk

Walk to the left from the front of the pub and cross the road past the post office. Go along the footway by the house with the Georgian portico, the old farm building with its central archway and the cottages, and reach the abbey and its adjacent shop. The fine wrought-iron gates are relatively modern (1959, and locally made) and carry the crest of the University of Oxford, which has appointed the vicars since 1557. The church, dedicated to St Mary (as all Cistercian churches), is what is left of an abbey founded in 1150 by Prince Henry, son of David I of Scotland, and settled by monks from Melrose – even the red sandstone was carried from Scotland. It was said the church was big enough for seven priests to say mass at once without interrupting each other. Throughout the wars of the reigns of the first two Edwards (1272 to 1327) the abbey was raided often – Edward I, himself, was here in 1300 and 1307 and the army was quartered hereabouts for eight whole years. Robert the Bruce raided in 1319, despite the fact that his father, the Earl of Carrick, was buried in the church (the gravestone is still to be seen in the modern ambulatory). At the dissolution, in 1538, the parishioners petitioned to keep the church for their use and as a place of refuge. At that time it had a tower, but this fell in 1600. It will be obvious that the building still suffers from problems of rising damp. Old cottages, which had been built on the site of the cloisters, have been renovated. Some 200 yards along the road beyond the shop is

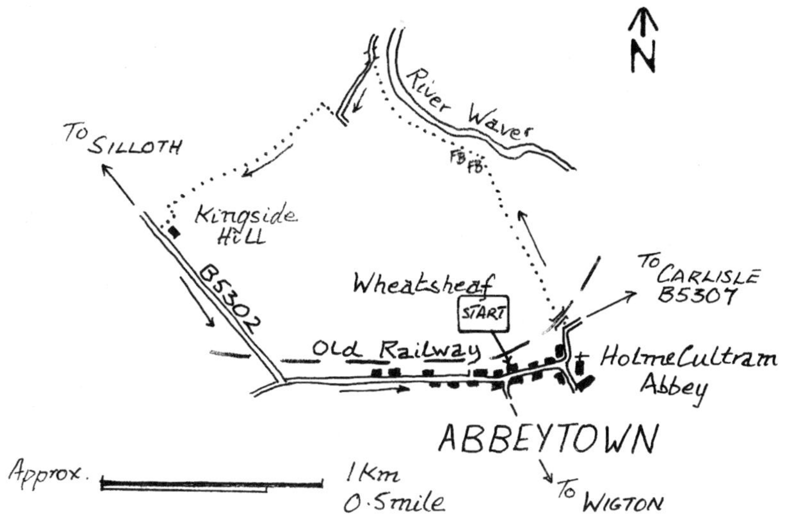

Mill Grove, which was once the abbey infirmary.

Exit the abbey grounds by the iron gate in the wall onto the Kirkbride road and walk round the bends, past Abbey Farm on the left, to turn left on the footpath at the corner and go under the arch of the abandoned railway. From 1856 to 1964 this carried the single track between Carlisle and Silloth. On the bend, continue ahead at the arrow marking the Cumbria Coastal Way and go through the steel gate into the field. Follow the left-hand boundary over the brow. Below lies the river Waver and across the far side is the large farm of Raby Cote (in the abbey porch is a record of the murder of Anne Musgrave at Raby Cote by one Robert Beckwith on 19 October 1586). Joseph Mann, of Raby, invented the first reaping machine, in 1826, and thereby changed the look of agriculture. Further in the distance are the masts of the radio station at Cardurnock and the hills of Dumfries. The field boundaries here are mainly earth banks topped with close-cut hedges and cattle churn up the mud in the gateways.

At the bottom of the slope go left over the stile and cross two footbridges, then walk along the bank of the tidal river. Perhaps surprisingly, otters have returned to these waters, and other nearby rivers, in recent years. Amongst the remains of the old hedge on your left are scattered gorse bushes which catch the morning dew on the gossamer of spiders' webs. Along the muddy water's edge oystercatchers probe. At the bend there is a stretch of sweet grass and some steps, hidden in the bank, lead up to a lane beside Rumbling Bridge. Turn left along the lane between hedges of elder, sloe, rose hips, damsons and cherries and walk to the next bend. Turn right, through the gate, on the footpath for Kingside Hill and go forward about 30 yards alongside a wire fence, then bear to the left round the corner and climb a slight rise. Here, I found a row of dead crows, hung up 'pour encourager les autres' – a rare sight, these days. Go left and right, past the galvanised water tank and continue, with the hedge on your right. Another uncommon experience in the late 20th-century countryside was when I put up a snipe from amongst the grasses. Aim for the farm buildings and go between the slurry tank and the right-hand barn (I found it very muddy just here) to exit to the main road.

Use the verge to walk back towards the village, looking out for the traffic. There are excellent views of the Skiddaw fells from the crest of the road. One section of the hedge, unusually, is entirely of gorse. At the bottom bend a signpost points to the delightfully named 'Aldoth' and 'Pelutho' – which could easily be somewhere in Tolkien's Middle Earth rather than everyday Cumbria. A footway starts at the stone-faced Victorian villas at the edge of the village. Walk past a shop, with a central entrance arch to a yard, the new school and the old Methodist church. The former school building, on the right, has a gable-end clock, like an oriel window, below the bell. Continue ahead at the turn of the road, back to the start.

18 Burgh by Sands
The Greyhound

Burgh (say 'Bruff') grew up on the site of the Roman fort of Aballava on the edge of the marshes where the river Eden flows into the Solway Firth at, more or less, the lowest practicable crossing point to the Scots shore. The long, straggling village street runs a wavering line between the vallum, the ditch, and Hadrian's Wall, on the northern side. The line of the vallum can be clearly seen at the back of the car park of the Greyhound. The pub is a fine, upstanding building in Georgian style which is set back from the roadside.

Food is available from 12 noon to 2 pm and 6.30 pm (7 pm on Sundays) to 8.30 pm (except for Thursdays). Sunday roasts are much sought after here and there is an extensive standard menu – the pies being ever popular. There are separate vegetarian and children's lists too.

This is a Greenalls house and their Bitter, Mild and Original are on draught, together with Younger Scotch ale. Stout is Guinness, lagers are both Tennents and Labatt's and the cider is Strongbow. There is a pleasant beer garden between the road and the front of the pub and a garden area for the children. Dogs are not permitted inside during food service times.

Telephone: 01228 576579.

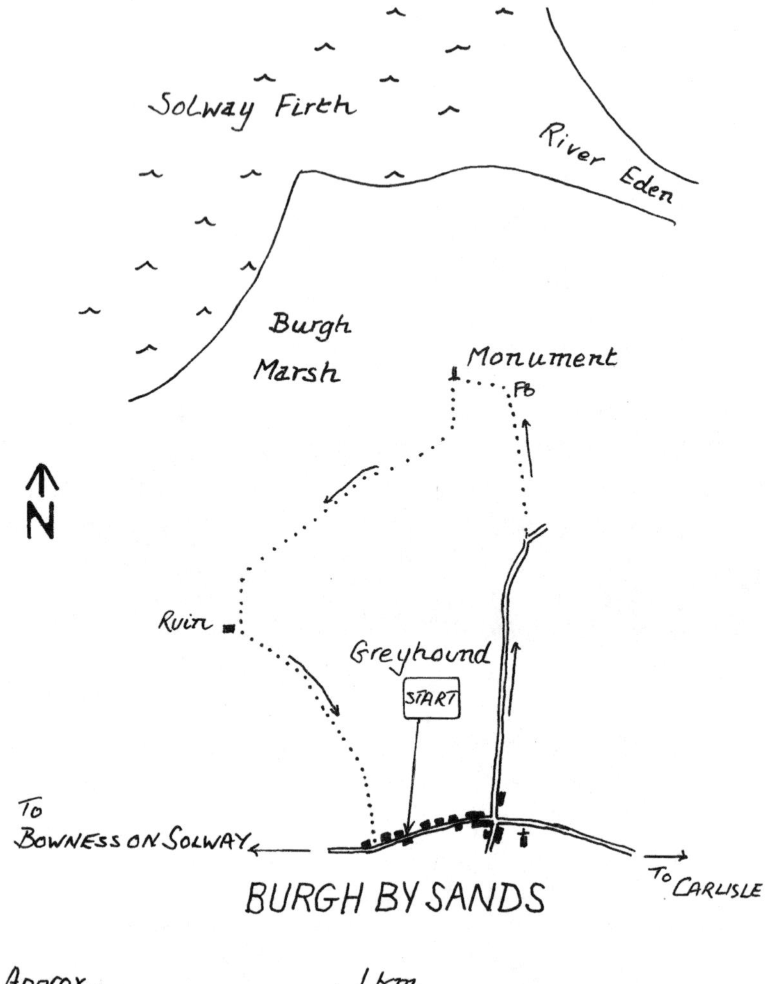

Solway Firth
River Eden
Burgh
Marsh
Monument
FB
N
Ruin
Greyhound
START
To
BOWNESS ON SOLWAY
To CARLISLE
BURGH BY SANDS
Approx.
1 km
0·5 mile

How to get there: Burgh by Sands is reached from the B5307 Abbeytown road west of Carlisle castle and taking the first right through Kirklandrews on Eden.

Parking: There is parking at the pub, but please ask at the bar when you wish to leave your car while you walk. A small amount of additional parking exists beside the church.

Length of the walk: 3½ miles. Map: OS Landranger 85 Carlisle (pub GR 324590).

The historic associations with the Romans and the Scottish wars are strong at Burgh. The walk, which is easy going underfoot, leads over the low brow to the Solway marshes, with their plentiful birdlife, and there are excellent views across the firth.

The Walk

Leave the pub in the direction of Carlisle and walk along the village street. Burgh House has a fine fan-light over the doorway and the brick and stone barn at Buckbottom Farm is exceptional. On the left is a superb thatched cottage with buttresses. Despite the existence of the already worked stone from the Roman buildings, many of the older cottages in the area are made of what is locally known as 'clay daubins' (wattle and daub) with cruck timbers for support. A couple of oddities of village history are that tobacco was once processed here and that it was the venue for horse races in Stuart times.

Continue as far as the church of St Michael. Most of its stones came from the Roman wall and it is one of three in Cumberland built with a defensive tower (14th-century and with walls 7 ft thick) with arrow slits and which has no doorway to the outside. The inside door still has its original iron gate. The upper section of the church tower was renewed in part in the late 1700s. Some of the masons' marks inside also appear on stones in Carlisle Cathedral and at Holme Cultram Abbey, Abbeytown (see Walk 17). The churchyard has a remarkable collection of Victorian decorated tombstones.

Retrace your steps to the crossroads and turn for Sandsfield by Cross Farm, with its fine covered gateway to the yard. Beyond the modern flats is another buttressed and thatched cottage. Walk out, over the brow, past the large, black corrugated barn on the right and over a second low brow. At the bend, turn left on the path along the right-hand of the two tracks. Drop steadily down, between fields of grain, to a double stile, footbridge and ditch which leads you out onto the marsh. Ahead is the Scottish shore, with Criffel standing out half-left and, in the immediate foreground, the monument to Edward I. Walk over the riggs and furrows of the marsh to view it from the western side of the iron fence. Edward died here, encamped on the marsh, on 7 July 1307, having made slow progress from Lanercost (see Walk 25) because of illness. The first monument was not erected until 1685 (by the Duke of Norfolk); it was rebuilt in 1803 (by the Earl of Lonsdale), restored in 1876 and more recently renovated once again and a new plaque set up. The marsh is National Trust property and is grazed by cattle and sheep. The parallel grooves ensure better drainage. Because of the wildfowl which come here in the winter the marshes, and the firth, are a reserve. A tidal bore rushes up the firth and is said to move faster than a horse can gallop. Even in recent times the old rectangular haaf nets have still been used to catch salmon.

Go directly south-west towards the fence line and walk along it to cross a rough farm culvert over a beck. Aim now for the nearest tall trees and a gate which has a tall footpath-marking post with a yellow top. Do not cross. Continue along the marsh side of the boundary, beside the drainage ditch overhung with trees and roses and with foxgloves on the bank. Out on the marsh you will surely see, and hear, curlews, oystercatchers and skylarks. Pass the dog-leg of the fence with the thick, heavy post and continue by two fields to the wooden steps and stile in the corner, where the hedge line swings to your right and rises a little as it does so.

Over the stile, continue along the left-hand boundary and up and over to drop to the remains of a group of Second World War buildings at the old firing range. Go straight through and bear half-left on the far side to the top left-hand corner of the field (use neither the track straight ahead nor the one to the left) to find a stile below an ash tree. Cross straight over the field to a stile by the steel gate and follow the green lane between high hedges, with long, narrow fields running at right-angles on the left. This returns you to the village street, opposite the bus stop (there is no sign here). At the back of the houses is the line of Hadrian's Wall (see also Walks 24 and 25). The Greyhound is 50 yards to the left.

19 Caldbeck
The Oddfellows Arms

Caldbeck lies at the extreme northern edge of the Lake District National Park and has given its name to the range of lower fells lying to the north of Blencathra and Skiddaw which are, for ever, associated with John Peel. For how long fox-hunting on foot has been practised in the area it is quite impossible to say, but it is clear that it long preceded the days of Peel (everyone knows the tune of the song which celebrates him – if not the right words!) and it still takes place, though the pack is based on the other side of Blencathra these days. The Oddfellows Arms stands on an island of roads to the south of the bridge and presents a bright, if unassuming, late 18th-century face to the passing world. The cosy inside still has the stone flags on its bar floor.

Food is available from 12 noon to 2 pm and 6.30 pm (7 pm on Sundays and in the winter) to 9 pm. Home-made steak and ale pie, roast duck, and chargrilled steaks are particularly popular and folk come here from miles about. For lighter meals, a variety of cold plates are complemented by sandwiches and jacket potatoes. Half portions are served for children and there is a vegetarian choice.

The bar of this freehouse is open all day on weekdays and Saturdays, and from 12 noon to 3 pm and 7 pm to 10.30 pm on Sundays. The draught beers are Jennings Bitter and Cumberland Ale, Younger Scotch ale and Fuller's ESB. The stout is Murphy's, the lager is Heineken, the cider Strongbow, and wine is on tap. There is a small beer garden. Dogs are permitted in the bar. Overnight accommodation is also available.

Telephone: 01697 78277.

How to get there: Caldbeck is situated on the B5299, which runs between Carlisle and Aspatria. It can also be reached from the B5305 Wigton to Penrith road. The pub is south of the bridge over the beck.

Parking: Some parking is available at the pub and there is a little adjacent roadside parking. A National Park car park is immediately to the north of the bridge over the beck.

Length of the walk: 3¼ miles. A shorter route, of 1½ miles, is also indicated on the sketch map. Map: OS Landranger 90 Penrith, Keswick and Ambleside (pub GR 324397).

The Caldbeck of today belies its industrial past – it had corn, woollen, bobbin and paper mills and a brewery, and the fells to the south were much mined. It is always associated with the huntsman John Peel. There is an ancient church and rural and mining museums. The limestone gorge of the Howk is most attractive and views over the common and fells in the latter part of the walk are wide.

The Walk

Leave the pub in the direction of Hesket Newmarket and Penrith and walk along the road to the church of St Kentigern, who is reputed to have preached here in the later 6th century AD. The present church is, essentially, based upon a foundation of the 12th century which was linked with Carlisle Priory. The interior is fine and bright and the arms of George IV (1820–30) still adorn the wall. A couple of medieval gravestones remain, one in the chancel – with a fine cross and sword inscribed on it – and one in the porch. Like many other churches in Cumbria, the tower is a later addition, here of 1727. Two graves in the churchyard are of interest. That of John Peel (1776–1854, who actually came from Ruthwaite, by Uldale, to the south-west) is by the wall, west of the south door, and is red sandstone, painted white. The famous song was penned by a local mill manager, John Woodcock Graves, and John's 'coat so grey' was actually woven in the mill beside the 'cold beck'. Mary Harrison, the 'Beauty of Buttermere' (see Walk 8), lies here too. Exit from the churchyard by the gate next to the small stone hut in the east wall and turn along the unmade lane to the left.

Beside the beck is the conglomeration of buildings known as Priests

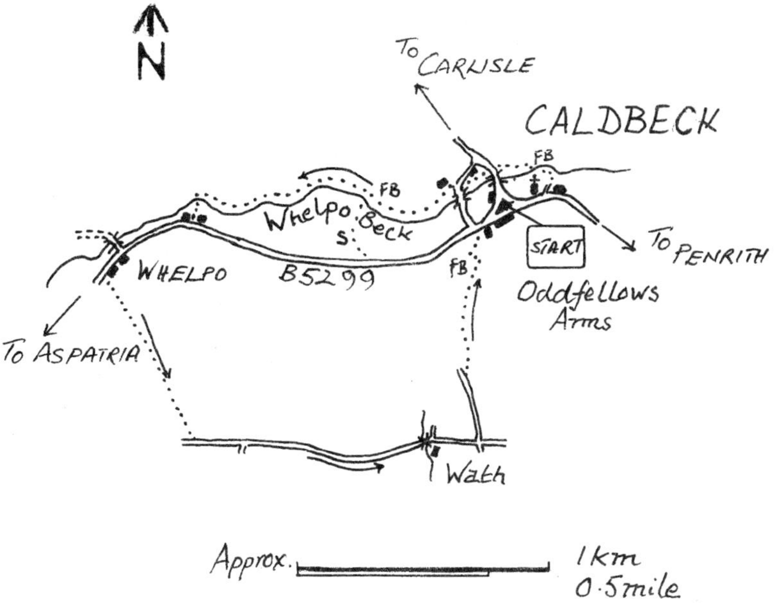

Mill. The restaurant is open all year, except for January, the shops and museum from March to October (except Mondays) and at weekends in November and December. Built in 1702, the mill used a 14 ft diameter wheel to grind corn until 1933. From then until 1965 it was a sawmill. Restoration was in 1986 and there are two museum areas. One, by the wheel, deals with the mill and has a collection of rural tools, the other relates the story of the mines of the area.

Leave across the car park and walk up the beck, past the steps to the holy well, as far as the footbridge and cross to the other bank. Continue, passing over the road and into the National Park car park. Exit to the right at the far end, bear up to the green and turn round to the left. Go straight ahead, between the barn and the house, at Bridge End Stables on the footpath for The Howk. Pass a ruined building to the right and two very large lime trees to reach double kissing-gates which lead onto a track. To the left is the chimney of one of the dozen or so mills which once operated in Caldbeck. The track leads into the wooded limestone gorge of the Whelpo beck. There is a rich growth of flowers in season – bluebells, celandines, red campions, forget-me-nots, wild garlic. Right in the middle of the entrance to the gorge are the ruins of Mary Mill (1857), which made bobbins with power provided by a 42 ft waterwheel. Use the steps up the right-hand side and walk above the potholes, caves and waterfalls of the gorge itself. A footbridge, at the head of the gorge, provides a short route back if desired (marked 'S' on the sketch map). The whole area of the Howk is now in the care of the National Park Authority.

The path now follows the unfenced beck bank through fields, with plenty of spots to sit and soak up the peace and tranquillity in the shade of alder and thorn. At the concrete farm bridge cross over and walk towards the large farm buildings of Beckstones. You have a choice of exiting to the road through the yard or bearing a little left and using a stile over the wall. Continue up the valley to the large stone arch of Whelpo bridge on the right. The cottage to the left was once a Quaker Meeting House (1698). Beyond the woodturner's shop and the farm of Swaledale Watch, go left over the stile by the modern barn and up the track, using the stiles beside the gates, to eventually continue on the line between the fence and the remains of an old hedge. At last, climb steadily up a long field to a stile to the lane. Behind is a view across Caldbeck Common and before you lie the fells in which mining for lead, copper and barytes began in the 13th century. The last mine closed in about 1960.

Turn to the left and pass a small shelter plantation and the lane to Fellside and Branthwaite. Ignore the footpath to the left and drop down the hill into the valley of the Gill beck. Ahead lie a couple of wind generators on the skyline and, nearer at hand, the pudding-shaped Mickle How. Go over the bridge at Wath, then continue for 200 yards to the crossroads and turn left down the narrow lane. Ignore the first footpath to the right and continue a further 50 yards to use the stile to the right (not the field gate or small gate). Aim to the right of the white house and use the stile and stone stile to cross a track. On the far slope are plantations of Scots pine and larch. Follow the left-hand boundary and find the stile behind the telegraph pole, then drop steeply down the bank to a footbridge and cross the beck below the broken mill weir. Bear round the garden of the house with the mill wheel. Pass a small new development on the right and go through to the steps up to the B5299 and turn right. On your right is a working blacksmith and, above, the great rarity of a clog-maker. Walk ahead to return to the pub.

20 Mungrisdale
The Mill Inn

The parish of Mungrisdale lies on the eastern edge of the Skiddaw and Blencathra fells. The name tells us that our Viking ancestors kept pigs here (there are other Grisdales in Lakeland) close by a church dedicated to St Mungo (the Scots familiar name for St Kentigern). It is but a tiny settlement and the inn lies across the bridge, inside the curve of the Glenderamackin (which may mean, simply, the river of the valley of the pigs in the old Celtic tongue), at the southern end. The range of buildings, of which the inn is the right-hand end, is typical of Lakeland fell farms with old and low beams internally and an open fire. There can be little doubt that it has stood here for more than 400 years. Dickens and Wilkie Collins stayed at the Mill during their visit to the area in 1857 and overnight accommodation is still available. The inn, itself, stands at around 750 ft above sea level. Where the car park now is was the village forge until the 1970s.

Food service hours are from 12 noon to 2 pm and 6 pm to 9 pm. The menu offers a wide choice. To catch the local mood, farmhouse pork pâté would make a good starter, before home-made meat pie. Roast duck and steaks are especially popular. There is a larger than usual vegetarian selection and a children's menu. Salads, sandwiches and baked potatoes are among the lighter offerings.

On weekdays and Saturdays the bar is open all day from 11 am to 11 pm, and coffee is served in the mornings. A freehouse, Jennings Traditional and Cumberland Ale, and Tetley Mild and Bitter are on draught. The stout is Guinness, lager is Heineken and cider is Strongbow. There is a family area and the dining room is non-smoking. Outside you will find a fine beer garden, overlooking the beck. Dogs are welcome.

Telephone: 017687 79632.

How to get there: Turn northwards at the sign from the A66 between Keswick and Penrith, west of the A5091 (Troutbeck) junction.

Parking: At the pub, by the road across the Glenderamackin, and a few spaces by the church.

Length of the walk: 5 miles. Map: OS Landranger 90 Penrith, Keswick and Ambleside (inn GR 363302).

The route enters the edge of the Blencathra group of fells and rises slowly to 1,623 ft on Souther Fell. Views towards the central and western Lakes are excellent and the middle valley of the Glenderamackin is a lonely and tranquil spot. It is absolutely necessary to be prepared for bad weather here.

The Walk

Turn right from the door and leave the car park along the lane to the gate across the road. The conical fell, half-left, is Great Mell. In 100 yards, by a small rocky knoll opposite some larches, pick up the start of a faint path to the right which leads, in 50 yards, to a definite track angling steadily up the flank of Souther Fell – there is no sign. (The National Park has in excess of 1,200 miles of public rights of way and at least the same length of permissive paths over the fells; this is of the latter sort.) The way becomes clearer and the view opens up to the south across Matterdale Common to the eastern side of the Helvellyn ridge. Snow lies late up in the combs and it is not unusual still to see it in June.

Eventually rise above the bracken to the sound of the meadow pipits and, perhaps, the occasional sparrowhawk and rarer peregrine – beside the path lie the inevitable sheep bones. It was somewhere up here, in the summer of 1744, that two local men saw horsemen galloping across a slope on which they knew no horse could keep a footing. No one believed their story until, at 7 pm on 23 June 1745, many of the local people saw the spectre of a troop of horsemen marching over the fellside. The scene lasted several hours. The occurrence was well documented and it was assumed to be the remnants of the defeated Jacobite army – but they were nowhere in

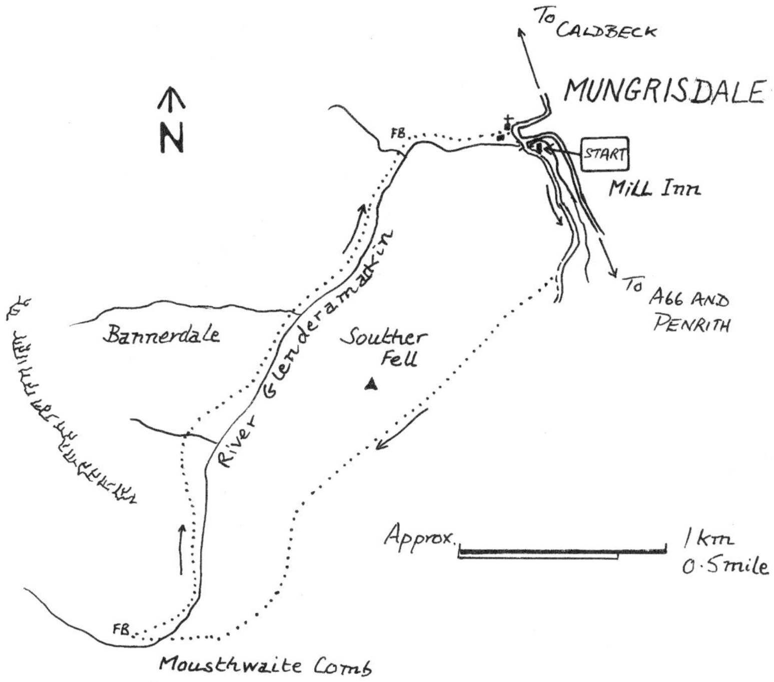

the vicinity at the time! How this could have come about no one has satisfactorily explained.

Almost at the ridge, the path becomes obscured again in a patch of bracken. Work gently through it and up to the ridge itself to join a clear path along the top. Aim for the low, peaty hause with a cairn of stones 100 yards to the right and a knoll to the left. Directly ahead is a view towards the summit of Blencathra and, across the valley, is the long line of Bannerdale Crags. Follow the ridge path over the knoll and take the right fork of paths. From this side, you are now looking towards Scafell, beyond Borrowdale, with Threlkeld quarries down below to the left. Aim down to the hause at the head of Mousthwaite Comb, below Scales Fell. Bear right down to the bridge over a much younger Glenderamackin.

Once across the beck, turn down the valley. The Glenderamackin cascades down, through a tiny wood of rowans, below the smooth, grassy slope of Souther Fell. At the crossing of the Bannerdale beck the view is east, out over Penrith and the Eden valley, to the Pennine ridge. As you slowly descend, the facing slope of the far side of Bullfell beck becomes more prominent, with its craggy slope scattered with juniper bushes and higher, towards Bowscale Fell, is a wide sweep of heather, purple in late summer. Join the track from the left, which comes over from the headwaters of the river Caldew, and cross the footbridge. There is another dramatic view behind you now to Bannerdale Crags. Walk off the fell, through two gates, past a house named Bannerdale View, and join the lane by the church. The little church of St Kentigern was built in 1756 to replace an older building. Coleridge records that two local Quakers, Isaac Ritson and John Slee, carried off the bell and buried it, sending their neighbours away to look for it in all the wrong places. Close to the bridge, in 1803, the Wordsworths and Coleridge nearly came to grief when their horse backed up the bank. A further connection with Wordsworth is the memorial tablet in the church to Raisley Calvert, who Wordsworth had nursed through illness. It was Calvert who left the poet the, then, considerable sum of £900 at a time when Wordsworth's fortunes were at a particularly low ebb. Turn right along the lane and right again over the bridge to return to the inn.

21 Wreay
The Plough Inn

Being only a few miles south of the city centre of Carlisle, Wreay (pronounced Ree-ah) hardly seems today the 'remote place by the bend of the river' its old Norse name suggests. It is, however, an exceedingly pretty place with some fine stone cottages and a unique church. The Plough Inn has been by the side of the road since at least 1664. There have been various additions to the building during the years, but it has a charming wholeness both inside and out. Interestingly, it is still the meeting place of the Twelve Men of Wreay. A self-electing body, which predated the establishment of parish councils, they continue to meet annually to carry out what small amount of business remains to them these days.

Lunchtime food is served between 12 noon and 2 pm and the menu is chalked up daily, examples being the unusual starter of corn-on-the-cob, followed by tuna and pasta bake. The selection is good and there are lighter meals and snacks available, such as ploughman's lunches, sandwiches and burgers. There is a children's menu and vegetarians are catered for. On Monday to Thursday evenings service is between 7 pm and 8.30 pm, on Fridays and Saturdays it is from 6.30 pm to 9 pm and on Sundays from 7 pm to 9 pm.

The bar is open all day from 11 am. Walker, Tetley and Calder's bitters are complemented by Tetley Mild at this freehouse. The stout is Guinness, lagers are Carlsberg and Castlemaine, and Gaymer's Old English cider is on draught. There is an attractive beer garden between the inn and the car park in which to enjoy sunny days. Dogs are not permitted.
Telephone: 016974 73504.

How to get there: From the M6 at junction 42 turn south off the Dalston road to reach Wreay, or approach the village from the A6, signed from Causeway House.

Parking: At the inn or beside the village green.

Length of the walk: 4½ miles. Map: OS Landranger 85 Carlisle (inn GR 436488).

The walk falls into two clear parts. The church, and associated structures, are of outstanding and unique interest. The valley of the river Petteril is secluded woodland which is a nature reserve well worth visiting.

The Walk

Cross over the road from the inn door and turn right for a few paces to the public footpath map board provided by the parish at the corner. Turn round left to the little green and cross over again to the church of St Mary, the third to be on the site. Built in 1842, this is based upon the design of a Roman basilica and was entirely designed by Sarah Losh, the exceptionally talented daughter of John Losh, of Woodside, as a memorial to her sister Catherine. The sisters had made the Grand Tour of Europe in about 1817 and Sarah incorporated an exuberance of allusions to this inside the building, which it is well worth spending time to investigate. The wood carving of the west door (created by her gardener), for example, depicts a gourd being eaten by a caterpillar, and much of the stonework was done by the local mason. The alabaster font was carved by Sarah herself. Externally, there are interesting gargoyles. Just outside the door are an imitation well and a sundial. Sarah and Catherine are buried together in the family enclosure in the far corner of the churchyard. Close by is a mausoleum in which a seated figure of Catherine sits holding a pine cone (symbol of eternal life) and the copy of the Bewcastle cross is a memorial to Sarah's parents (the real one, of late 7th-century AD date, stands in the churchyard of Bewcastle, some 20 miles away, in the far north-eastern corner of the county). The school and the school house also owe their existence to Sarah Losh. Exit to the Carlisle lane from the churchyard by following the flagged path on the far side of the building.

Cross over past the telephone box and go left for 50 yards to the

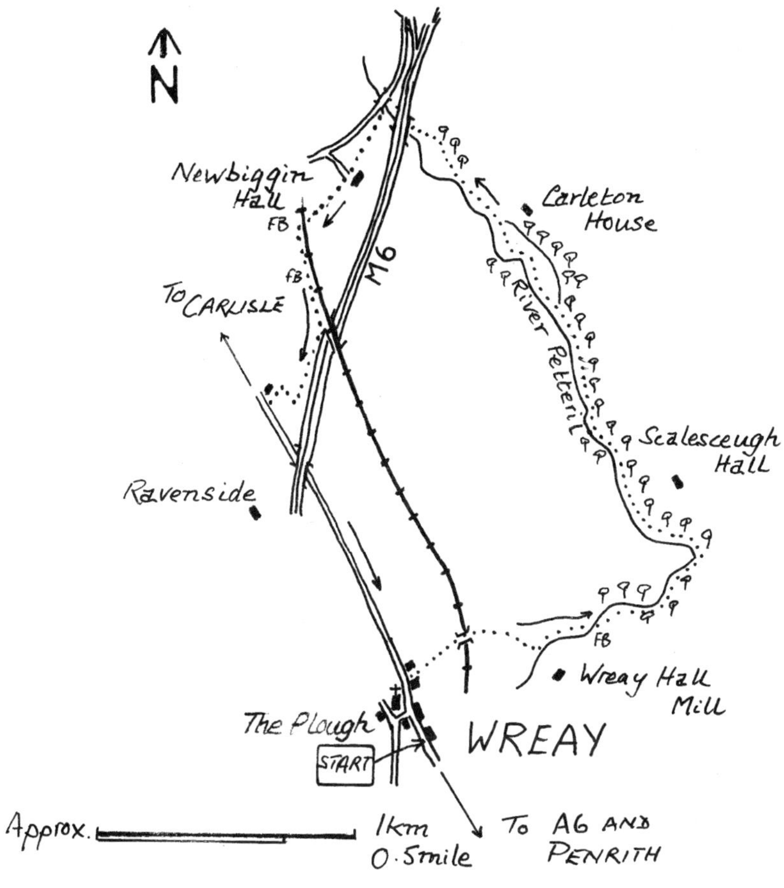

footpath for Newbiggin. Pass the old cottage of Wreay Syke on the left. Walk along the metalled lane. The view left, on a clear day, is up Liddesdale, beyond the Scottish border. Closer is the tower of Border TV, in Carlisle centre, and half-right the Pennine ridge dominates but, on the nearest hillock, lie the remains of a Roman signal station. Go down, in the shade of oak and beech, and cross the bridge of the main London to Glasgow railway, taking the footpath to the right off the bend. Follow the right-hand boundary down into the valley and bear downstream at the bottom to a green metal footbridge over the limpid water of the river Petteril, north of Wreay Hall Mill. Turn left to enter the woodland.

At the crossing of the fence you enter the Wreay Woods reserve of the

Cumbria Wildlife Trust. The mixed woodlands on both banks of the river contain a wide variety of species of tree, largely as a result of extensive felling in the early 1970s – oak, beech, holly, rowan, ash, sycamore, hawthorn, willow, alder, poplar and rhododendron all crowd together. The ground flora is typical of mixed woodlands but in spring includes the rarer moschatel (town hall clock) with its head of five outward-facing, pale green flowers. Growth is lush with ferns, goosegrass and bramble rioting everywhere in their season. Through the woods the river cascades over the rocks on which traces of visiting otters can occasionally be found. Fallen logs indicate how powerful the wintertime flow can be. From time to time there are long, slow pools, dappled by rising fish. Along the banks are stunning displays in June of the garden escapee called dame's violet. In summer sun, insects fill the air with a constant hum and butterflies flit in and out of the patches of light. Birdlife is plentiful, with dippers hunting the river for insects and blackcaps to be found in the shrub layer between April and September. Keep down by the water (do not go right up the steps – this leads to Scalesceugh Hall). The path is diverted at one point because of bank erosion. Eventually, the wood thins out with bracken and summertime willow herb and stitchwort in the clearings. Pass a small side gorge, to the right, with a waterfall and reach a stile into fields.

The path runs clear across the grass and below Carleton House, up on top of the right-hand bank. At the far end is a steel gate and a stile. After a second stile in 100 yards, follow the path along the wood edge to a slight bend. Bear off at right angles over the field to go under a motorway bridge over the river and reach a picnic site beside the Dalston lane. Walk to the left over the bridge – the old one remains next to it – and along the lane to reach the access of Newbiggin Hall. This once belonged to Carlisle Priory and is built round a defensive pele tower.

Turn along the access track and keep right of the cottages and the modern barn to a stile, then walk ahead over a horrid, corrugated iron bridge back over the railway. At the far kissing-gate go to the left beneath a large beech tree and drop down to cross the Woodside beck by a footbridge; the bank up again is muddy. Follow the signs around the edge of the field to reach a gate between Low Hurst farm and the motorway maintenance depot. A little along the road to the right is Woodside, the Losh property, where Wordsworth was often entertained. Turn left, however, and walk along the verge, under the motorway and over the brow beside a belt of trees. Pass Ravenside Lodge and re-enter the village past the church and the telephone box.

22 Wetheral
The Wheatsheaf Inn

The village of Wetheral has, even today, still managed to evade the clutches of spreading Carlisle but it is, in the main, a dormitory for the city. The consequence is that it is well kept and well serviced. The Wheatsheaf is, for certain, an old building and has been there since the 15th century. Its interior retains an old-world atmosphere and appearance.

Food is available in the middle of the day between 12 noon and 2 pm and from 6.30 pm to 8.30 pm each evening. The menu is varied, with a high proportion of home-made meals. I wonder if the lamb chops still come from the wethers folded on the haugh – young, castrated rams grazing by the river – for this is the meaning of the village name. They certainly make a fine follow on to home-made soup on a crisp autumn day. There is an international flavour to many dishes, without there being a take-over. The vegetarian menu is short but interesting and salads and sandwiches will suit the lighter eater. There is a separate children's menu.

On Monday to Friday the bar is open from 12 noon to 3 pm and 6 pm to 11 pm. Saturday is all day opening from noon, and Sunday is similar but, of course, the bar closes at 10.30 pm. A Greenalls house, Mild and Thomas Greenall's Original Bitter are on draught. Stout is Guinness, the lager is Labatt's and ciders are Dry Blackthorn and Woodpecker. Wines are served at the bar and by the bottle and there is a special 'Malt of the Month'. The beer garden between the pub and car park is very attractive indeed, and summertime hanging baskets decorate the building itself. Dogs are welcome in the garden but are excluded from the pub during food serving hours.

Telephone: 01228 560686.

How to get there: The village lies on the B6263 between the M6 at junction 42 and the A69 at Warwick Bridge. It is due east of Carlisle city and can also be reached from there through Scotby or Harraby. The pub is on the bend at the southern end of the village. There is a station on the Carlisle to Newcastle line.

Parking: At the pub and by the roadside next to the green. Please check at the bar before leaving your car in the pub car park while you walk.

Length of the walk: 3 miles. A diversion across the river to Great Corby and its castle will add about 2 miles. Map: OS Landranger 86 Haltwhistle, Bewcastle and Alston (pub GR 464542)

This walk combines a fine riverside walk through attractive woodland with a visit to the unique church and the remains of Wetheral Priory. Except for the short climb up from the river it is easy going underfoot. There is an opportunity to divert across the bridge to Corby on the far bank.

The Walk

Turn in the direction of Warwick Bridge and walk along the footway towards the green, passing the village hall of 1891 and rows of red sandstone cottages. Keep on the top side of the green and pass several Victorian villas, one of which is now the headquarters of the county probation service. Bear to the right by the post office and follow the sign for the station. The Crown Hotel has a fine Georgian porch with Ionic columns. At the station, it is possible to divert across the line and use the footbridge, which parallels the railway, over the river Eden to Great Corby and look at Corby Castle. Otherwise, turn down the Ninetynine Steps (a slight underestimate I think!) to the road along the river below. Up above are the five arches of the railway bridge. Walk past the newish houses in the old quarry and bear up to the right (there is no sign) beyond Edenside House to enter the churchyard through an iron gate.

Holy Trinity, St Mary and St Constantine, where 900 years of worship were celebrated in 1988, is the only church in the country with a dedication to the latter saint who, so tradition has it, sheltered in caves by the river here. What you see now is essentially 16th century. A mausoleum

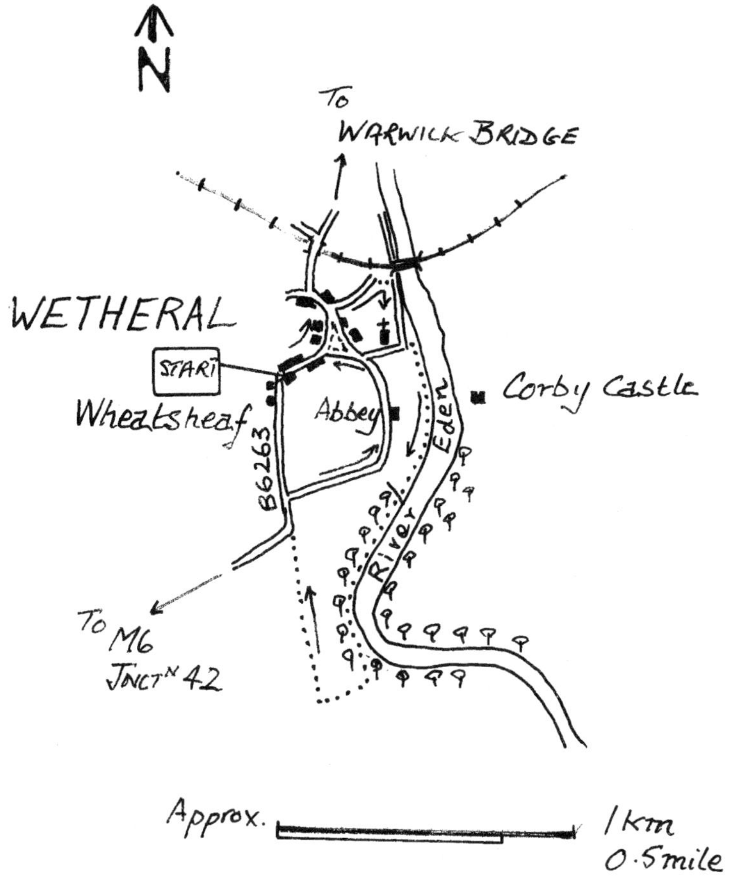

for the Howards of Corby was added in 1791 and there is a group memorial to Lady Maria Howard, done by the sculptor Joseph Nollekens at about the same date and entitled *Faith*. It is one of his finest works and Wordsworth was inspired to write a sonnet about it. Leave the church on the far side through the lychgate and turn downhill, past Ferry Hill House, to the river bank. Until the railway came, in 1830, this was the crossing of the river – it cost a whole penny each.

Go right, through the picnic area, and up the slow flowing river on the path along the bank. The woods around Corby Castle set off its formal Italianate gardens which decorate the cliff down to the river on the far side. It will be worth stopping to view them at several places as you progress – there are caves, archways, steps and a life-size statue of St Constantine.

The sandy path wanders amongst lime trees, sycamore, elm and ash and shortly takes the stone steps up to the right beside the field to avoid the floods. Blackberries and raspberries in season grow in profusion beside the way. At the far end of the field, enter the National Trust property of Wetheral Woods, noting the warning sign that the path can be slippery when wet. Gradually climb up with the main path until it joins an old track coming in from your right, more or less opposite the weirs on the far side of the river. Cross over the track and continue up a little under large beech trees (ignore the stile on the right). Follow round the bend of the river at this higher level and slowly swing and drop down to river level once more. Within the woods are St Constantine's caves – if you can locate them. At last, pass a ruin of a corrugated-roofed hut on the right. In 25 yards turn right up the bank before you reach the footbridge. Enter fields by the stile at the top.

Go immediately right through the steel gate and turn left along the boundary to the corner beyond the oak tree. Turn at right angles to your right and cross the field to an iron kissing-gate and continue ahead on the left-hand boundary to a second kissing-gate onto the B6263. Through the trees, across the river, the massive lion, with its tail outflung, on the top of Corby Castle, should be visible. Go to the right along the verge for a few yards and turn right along the lane beside the sports field. At the bend there is an even finer view across to the castle. Drop along the lane to the Priory Gatehouse. This is looked after by English Heritage and is freely open to view. It is all that is left of the Benedictine Priory, founded in 1106 by Ranulph de Meschines for monks from St Mary's Abbey at York. It was in use as the vicarage until the 18th century and is, consequently, well preserved. There is even a spiral stair to roof level. Information panels give the details on site. Return to the lane and continue round, past The Glebe, then bend back up to the green, past the cross, to return to the pub.

23 Blackford
The Metal Bridge Inn

Standing beside the southern approach to the bridge over the river Esk, the Metal Bridge Inn is probably one of the most easily located, and most often seen, pubs in the county – if not the whole North of England. Its postal address is, however, somewhat confusing for it stands in Rockliffe parish, close to the boundary with Westlinton parish, which the village of Blackford happens to lie on the far side of. Confusion is further confounded by the expectation, the first time you pass this way, that this must be the Scottish border but this lies 2 miles further on, on the edge of Gretna, at the trickle of the river Sark. The land between the two rivers was once known, nationwide, as the 'Debatable Land'. The Metal Bridge Inn has looked out across it in peace for 150 years and more. The older parts of the building were, quite clearly, a farm and the inside is set at several levels. A modern addition has been a conservatory dining area cantilevered out over the river.

Food is served from 12 noon to 2.30 pm (coffee is available from 11 am) and between 5.30 pm and 9.30 pm. Evening service on Sundays is from 7 pm to 9 pm. On the standard menu, the turkey stir-fry is very popular, and the roll-mop herrings and Northumbrian hotpot attract many customers when they are on the specials board. Vegetarians, the lighter eater and children are all well catered for.

This is a Scottish and Newcastle house and has their own ales on draught, including Theakston BB. The stout is Guinness, the lager is, of course, McEwan's, and the cider is Dry Blackthorn. Bar hours are from 11 am to 11 pm (10.30 pm on Sundays). The conservatory is a non-smoking area and here, and in the alcove, families are particularly welcome. Outside there is a pleasant beer garden. Dogs are welcome except in the food service areas. Overnight accommodation is also available.

Telephone: 01228 74206.

How to get there: Exit from the A74 dual carriageway at signs for the special slip roads on the south bank of the river Esk.

Parking: At the pub, but please tell someone at the bar if you are leaving your car while you walk.

Length of the walk: 4½ miles. Map: OS Landranger 85 Carlisle (inn GR 355648).

This quiet and peaceful countryside beside the estuary of the Esk and the Solway marshes belies a turbulent history. Sea and marsh birds are of special interest. Much of the route is along lanes, is virtually flat and is very easy going underfoot.

The Walk

Turn to the left from the inn door and go left from the car park entrance to drop to the river level. Immediately above is the old buttress of the Metal Bridge itself. A plaque records that it was built in 1820, replaced by the Esk Bridge in 1915, and that has now been superseded by the modern concrete structure carrying the A74 from Carlisle to Glasgow. Use the footway under the bridge. (It was just here that I had the finest view of a common sandpiper. It sat on a fence post, in bright sunshine, within 2 ft of me and allowed me to walk slowly past!) Take the stile to the left at the corner, for Lynefoot, and walk along the river, upstream and through the old gravel works. What dominates today is the view – way up Eskdale – and the wildlife by the river, swans, shelduck, herons, a kestrel hovering and, maybe, an otter. Take your mind back, however, to a chill November morning in 1542 when Wharton, Lord of the West March and commanding only 3,000 English in Carlisle, saw the sky red with burning fires as 15,000 Scotsmen came south over the moss. The Scots vanguard was caught, quite literally, where you now stand, at the crook where Esk and Lyne meet, and thrown back across the river to be cut to pieces about a mile on the Scots side. Just seven English were killed. How many Scots is unknown – large numbers were drowned and 1,200 prisoners taken. It was

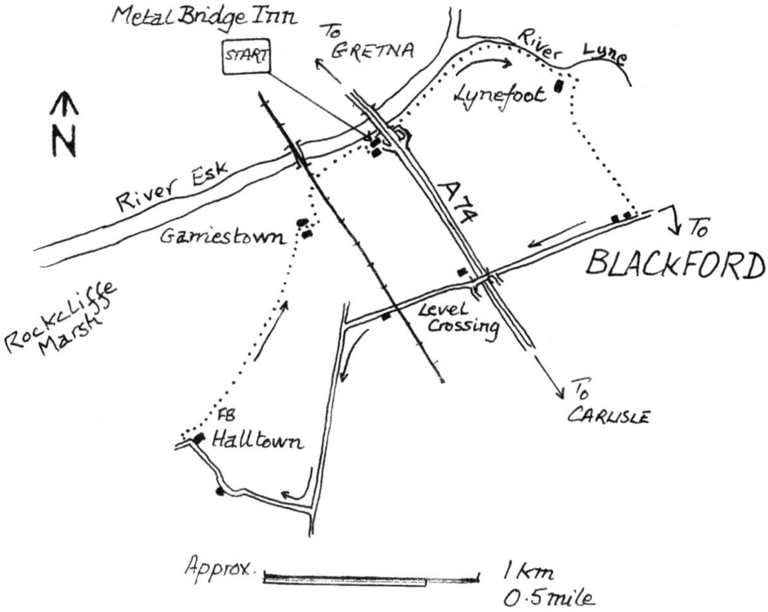

the worst rout ever suffered by any Scots army. It took another 11 years before agreement was finally reached over the division of the Debatable Land itself, when the English acquired the stretch north of the Esk and the Scots' Dike was built (where the border is now marked on the A7 to Langholm).

After all that excitement, go to the right, over the stile and up the river Lyne, with a view across the floodbank on the far side to the conifer plantations of Kershope on the hills in the distance. Continue along the upper bank to a stile by a knarled oak and drop down left, beside lime trees, going left of the garden of Lynefoot to a stile in the corner. Cross into the garden and follow the left-hand hedge to the access road and turn left. On the bend is a plantation of flowering cherry, horse chestnut and rhododendron – a riot of colour in early summer. Follow down the row of beeches and the barley field on the left and reach the road by Broomyknow. Turn right. The avenue of trees is now horse chestnuts. Continue along the verge to Floriston Bridge over the A74. The Dumfries hills stand out half-right and the northern fells of the Lake District are visible to the south. Pass by Floristonrigg, on the right, and some imported red sandstone gateposts to a field and cross over the main London–Glasgow line by the level crossing. A small cottage nestles in the wood to the left.

At the T-junction go to the left and walk down the verge past plantations of Scots pine and larch. The beech, on the right, is older and some of the individual scattered oak trees sport nest boxes. The ground vegetation is heathy with heather and gorse, and pheasants may be calling in the coverts. Pass beneath two power lines and turn to the right at the sign for Rockliffe Cross. Walk past the modern bungalow and the barns of Wether Hill at the bend to the brick house at Halltown, its gable hung with slates. On the bend a stile drops you awkwardly into the field on a path for 'Metal Bridge'. Ahead are the cooling towers of Chapel Cross power station and Criffel half to the left. Go right by the newly planted alders and over two stiles, then round the farmyard and ahead to a third stile.

In front, now, is Gretna village on its low rise. A footbridge takes you over Peter Sike with its red, sandy bottom. Keep beside the old hedge on the left and amongst rushes to a stile in the corner in a bed of nettles. Once in the field, follow the left-hand boundary, with crab apple trees in it, and join a green lane. Continue between hedges and gradually come to meet the sea bank of Rockliffe Marsh, which runs away to your left. Go back beneath the power lines and walk through the yard of the refurbished Garriestown, then go left along the track at the sign. The ditch below is overhung by old willow and wind-blown beech. At the meeting of the river bank and the railway, turn over the tracks with very great care and join the bank beside the tidal river Esk and its ever-wheeling gulls. Use the second gate to the right and follow the left-hand boundary, then dog-leg to a track between the house and the inn car park.

24 Laversdale
The Sportsman Inn

Laversdale is one of the small communities in the agricultural land east of Carlisle, which lies between the fertile Solway Plain and the gradually rising fells before they sweep up to the north-east corner of the county and the wild border with Scotland and Northumberland. Just north of the line of Hadrian's Wall, it is in the parish of Irthington. The Sportsman stands on the bend of the road at the northern end. Back in 1801 it was the blacksmith's and coffin maker's, by 1867 it was the Dog and Gun, and it got its present name as recently as 1958. The simple and straightforward outward appearance is wedded to a warm and welcoming interior.

Food is served from 11 am to 2.30 pm and 6 pm to 9.30 pm each day – you should check availability on winter lunchtimes. An unexpectedly popular offering is the home-made coleslaw with chips (with a more toothsome texture than the supermarket variety!). When the cold wind comes down over the Border, gammon and eggs keeps out the weather, and follows well a hot and filling home-made soup. There is a special children's menu and a vegetarian choice.

This is a Scottish and Newcastle house with both Scotch ale and Theakston BB on draught. The stout is Gillespies, lager is McEwan's and the cider is Dry Blackthorn. Wine is on tap. Bar hours are 11 am to 3 pm and 6 pm to 11 pm (10.30 pm on Sundays and bank holidays). There is a non-smoking area inside and the rear of the dining area is for family use. Adjacent to the beer garden is an area for children. Dogs are most welcome and they will find a refreshing bowl of water waiting.

Telephone: 01228 573255.

How to get there: Turn off the A6071 between Brampton and Longtown at the sign for Laversdale or approach from the A689, going northwards past the entrance to Carlisle airport.

Parking: At the inn – please ask at the bar if you want to park while you walk – or beside the small green across the road.

Length of the walk: 6 miles. Map: OS Landranger 86 Haltwhistle, Bewcastle and Alston (inn GR 476625).

This easy circuit links the villages Laversdale and Scaleby, across a shallow valley. Scaleby's church and castle are worth seeing and you return along a length of Hadrian's Wall.

The Walk

The walk starts immediately beside the inn on the footpath signed for Scaleby Mill. As you move into the broad, shallow valley in which 10th-century Leofhere settled, the light, sandy soil should be dry underfoot and the hedges filled with flowers in season – vetches, red dead nettle, stitchwort, violets, speedwells, even bluebells. Lean on the gate at the top of the rise and enjoy the wide view – from King's Forest of Geltsdale, in the Pennines to the south, to Blencathra in the northern Lakes, over the Solway to Criffel in Dumfries, and up to Kershope and the Border, northwards. The descent is gentle and grassy, past the barn of Bullersike, on the right, and down to the footbridge over the Highberries beck. Scaleby Mill is just right of the junction with the access track.

Go left towards Woodhead Farm and walk through, in front of the house, along a row of beech and to the gate to the right past the copper beech. Cross the boundary line at the gate and continue along the wire fence to swing left to a gate by a ditch and join a clear track. In 50 yards turn right on a track beneath another copper beech and follow it, with marshy fields to your left, to the road at Fordsyke. The house is of hand-made brick. Walk along the lane now, with care for traffic, and pass Scaleby Hall on the left and then the entrance to Scaleby Castle and continue to All Saints' church. This is early 13th century, much restored in 1861. Texts still hang on the walls and there is a fragment of a Roman altar. It has clearly been around a long time for a spot the name of which means 'the temporary settlement'. Leave the church past the little red sandstone

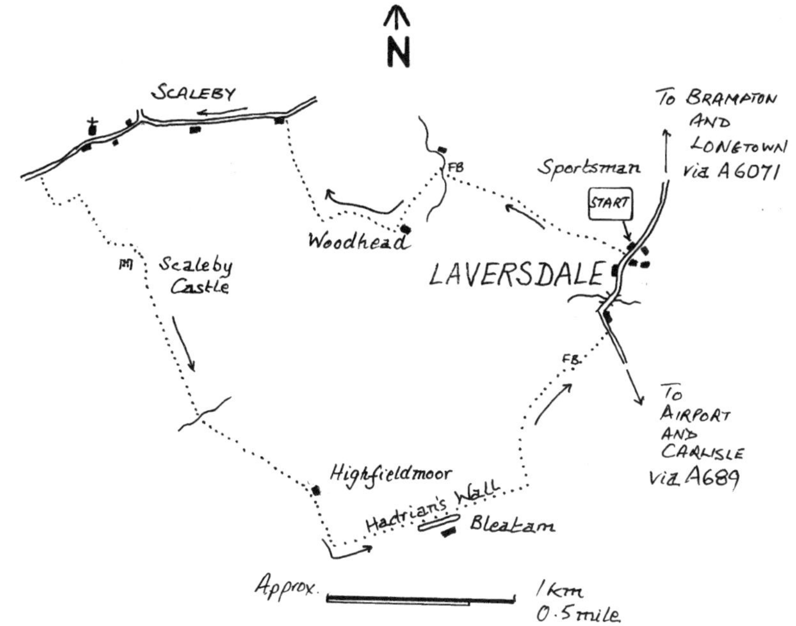

hall and go a further 300 yards to a footpath to the left for Hadrian's Wall, opposite the seat on the verge.

Follow the right-hand boundary to a stile and bear left through a belt of spruces to an iron up and over stile. Do not use it, but turn right on its nearside and go along the left-hand boundary beside a belt of oaks to a stile by the gate at the end of the field. Bear half-left, past the isolated pine, to the gate in the iron fence by the bridge over the moat to the castle. This remains a private residence and you will have to be content with what you can see through the trees. It dates from 1307 and the original defensive pele tower has been much added to down the centuries, within the confines of a perfectly circular moat.

Follow the footpath sign and continue to the far gate of the field ahead. Turn left along the boundary ditch through a rushy field, use the farm bridge over the drain and continue forward. This is curlew, lapwing and skylark country. Cross the Laversdale beck, with its stoned and strengthened banks, on a concrete bridge. Continue through the far gate and follow the right-hand boundary, of wire fence and old hedge, up two long fields to Highfieldmoor Farm. Go through the yard and cross to the track on the right by the new barns at the far side. Drop down a little and cross over Baron's beck at the junction with a concrete access road.

Turn left on the far side, past the cattle grid, and join the path along the line of Hadrian's Wall by the hedge of crab apples. Follow the ridge that marks the Wall line eastwards through the field. (This area, and those visited on Walks 18 and 25, are part of the Hadrian's Wall World Heritage Site.) Walk past Bleatarn (which is the site of a quarry for the Wall) and its farm, on the brow to the right and find the stile and gate which lead onto a grassy track beyond – this is an old drove road along the Wall line.

Go left and immediately right up the bank between the beech trees and over another stile, then follow along the left-hand boundary above the drove road with many bird-cherries in the hedge. Across to the right are the hangars of Carlisle airport. At the end of the field use the rather poor stile to the left (do not go ahead) and jump over the ditch. Just beyond this point is Milecastle 60 where the Sixth Legion erected an altar to Cocidius (which is now at Castlesteads). On the far side of the ditch, find a further stile and cross the field direct to another. Go over the next field to the gate and proceed diagonally right to a stile. Some 10 yards further on is a footbridge to the left. Follow the boundary to the lane and turn left to return via the village to the inn. You pass Stonewalls, the home of a famous local Cavalier, Randle Mulcaster, known as 'Randie of the Long Sword', who now lies buried in nearby Irthington.

25 Lanercost
The Abbey Bridge Inn

Lanercost is, today, but a hamlet not far from the crossing of the river Irthing. In so far as we know what the name means at all it seems to refer to a woodland glade. The Abbey Bridge Inn is at the southern end of the old bridge, in the shade of the trees of Tenterbank Wood so, perhaps, that interpretation still fits. Originally a forge and stables, the buildings began in the 1640s – no doubt much of the stone taken from the priory itself. In 1850 the farmhouse was converted to a hotel but, because of the teetotal views of the Countess of Carlisle, of Naworth, on whose estates it stood, it was not licensed until around 1960. The bar is, in fact, separate from the hotel building, across the yard in the old forge.

Food is served from 12 noon to 1.45 pm and between 7 pm and 8.45 pm every day. The à la carte menu is fine indeed. I've always been a great fan of deep fried whitebait (and it appears less frequently nowadays, it seems) so this, followed by a fillet steak in whisky, tomato and cream sauce, is a rare delight. Equally tempting would be the deep fried Brie, followed by venison casserole. Vegetarians will find an interesting choice too.

A freehouse, this has been voted the best real ale pub in the county. During the year a choice of up to 400 beers is on draught, with 15 to 20 each week for your enjoyment. Stout, lager and cider are available for the non-beer drinkers who can squeeze to the bar. Service times are 12 noon to 2.30 pm and 7 pm to 11 pm (10.30 pm on Sundays). The restaurant is a non-smoking area, and families are welcome. There is a pleasant beer garden. Dogs are welcome except in the dining areas.

Telephone: 016977 2224.

How to get there: The simplest approach is from the A6071, at the eastern end of Brampton town, from the green on which there is a large stone shelter, looking like a bandstand. Otherwise, turn from the A69 through Naworth, or turn from the B6318 west of Gilsland.

Parking: There is limited parking outside the inn which is mainly taken up by hotel residents. Across the old bridge from the inn, on a section of what used to be the road, there is an extensive public car park.

Length of the walk: 3½ miles. Map: OS Landranger 86 Haltwhistle, Bewcastle and Alston (hotel GR 553632).

A pleasant walk in, and above, the valley of the river Irthing. The route includes a section of Hadrian's Wall (see also Walks 18 and 24) and the beautiful priory at Lanercost. There is a moderate amount of climbing. Several other sites of interest are very close by.

The Walk

Find the footpath for Burtholme at the north end of the old bridge and go down onto the river bank. The two-arched bridge is medieval and most attractive when the sun catches the red sandstone – however, you will probably want to miss out its modern companion from any photograph! Go a few paces downriver to a gate on the right by a beech tree and cross to the far side of the field boundary, then keep with the left-hand boundary. This edges away from the river and leads you to an up and over stile. Walk up the field beside the small beck and past several old sycamore trees which have been protected by iron railings; now they have grown so large that the railings have broken and are enclosed in the bark of the trees. Walk through to the lane.

Turn to the left and pass the buildings of the farm hamlet of Burtholme. Continue past the row of trees, and the summertime roses in the hedge, as far as the second bend. There is a stile in the hedge on the left before the gate (no sign). Take this and follow the right-hand boundary round to a stile and footbridge over a ditch. Walk straight up the field past the isolated trees and aim to the right of the buildings of Howgill, then exit to the access lane. Go along this only as far as the first field boundary to the right. Turn through the gate (again no sign) and follow the left-hand boundary down into the dip where the cows have churned up the stream

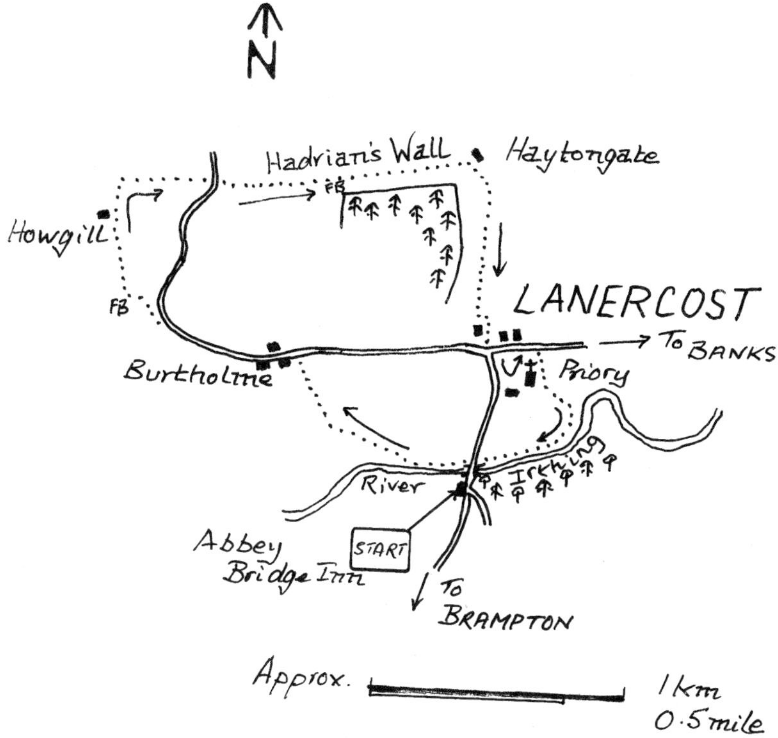

into a mud patch. Climb up past the two Scots pines and go left and right through the gateways at the field corner, then cross directly over the last field to a gate to a lane. Turn to the right and almost immediately go left on the footpath for Banks. The up and over stile is in poor repair. You have been on the line of Hadrian's Wall since Howgill but it becomes clearer here. Cross the field end and go through the kissing-gate and along the left-hand boundary, past the site of Turret 54A and drop to the Burtholme beck. Find the kissing-gate to the left and bear right to the footbridge, crossing the beck to a stile.

Climb up the bank, with the spruce plantation of Abbey Gills Wood on your right, and pass the site of Milecastle 54, at the flattened area on the way up. At the buildings of Haytongate, turn to the right and walk along the access track, following it down towards the valley. There is a very fine view of the whole priory site from here. At the corner of the road, with its old black and white signpost still in place and the bright-red stone of some modern houses on the left, go straight ahead and walk through the arch of the old gateway (only the inner arch remains) into the grounds of the priory. It was founded, as a house of Augustinian canons, in the 1160s. The Scots attacked it in 1296 and Edward I made it his headquarters during his final campaign of 1306–7. After the dissolution it came into the hands of the Dacre family and remained with them until 1716. The part they occupied is now the village hall and next to it the priory guest house remains intact. The church, dedicated to St Mary Magdalene, was restored as the parish church in the 17th century. The monastic buildings are in the keeping of English Heritage and are architecturally most interesting, the vaulted undercroft especially so.

Leave the grounds by going along the north side, past the old cross, to the white kissing-gate and through the graveyard to a second kissing-gate to the field, then take the footpath towards the river on the far side of the ruins. Follow the white posts to walk right along the river bank beside tea-brown water and shingle banks on which oystercatchers nest. Cross the road and go back over the old bridge to the inn.

Several other things of interest are so close you will, surely, wish to visit them. Up the road beyond the priory, through Banks, and towards Gilsland you will find the excavated remains of Banks Turret and Pike Hill Signal Tower on the Wall. Immediately across the road, in the field, is an extremely fine limekiln of much more recent vintage. Half a mile up the road opposite the inn is Naworth Castle. Still the home of the Earls of Carlisle, this is open on certain days of the week between Easter and the end of September (telephone: 016977 3666).

26 Hallbankgate
The Belted Will Inn

'Belted Will', or 'Bauld Willie', was Lord William Howard who married the heiress of the Lanercost estate (see Walk 25) in 1577. He got his epithet from the large and wide shoulder belt he often wore and earned fame in the tidying up of the depredations of the Border reivers in the first years of the reign of James I. Sir Walter Scott used him as a character in *The Lay of the Last Minstrel.* Like others on the Naworth estates, the pub was a temperance house when Rosalind, Countess of Carlisle held sway and was only licensed again in the 1970s when the interior received a face-lift in keeping with the times. The welcome is a good one and the stove ensures the bar is a warm and friendly place even when the cold winds blow over the Pennines from the east.

Food is served all day from 12 noon until 9.45 pm. The menu is simple and straightforward, with steak and onions being an ever popular choice. An international flavour is provided by a choice of curries, and lighter meals include salads, and baked potatoes with various fillings. Vegetarians will find a choice and children's portions are served. The sweet selection is unusually good.

This is a Tennents house and, in addition to their light ale, serves Joules Crown, and Worthington, Bass and Stones bitters. The stout is Guinness, the lager Tennents' own and the cider Dry Blackthorn. The bar is open all day from 11 am to 11 pm (10.30 pm on Sundays). Well-behaved dogs are welcome. Overnight accommodation is also available.

Telephone: 016977 46236.

How to get there: The pub is at the junction of the Brampton to Alston road (the A689) with the lane to Talkin, in the centre of the village.

Parking: There is a small amount of parking outside the pub itself and additional public parking across the way beside the lane to Clowsgill.

Length of the walk: 4¾ miles. Map: OS Landranger 86 Haltwhistle, Bewcastle and Alston (pub GR 580595).

The quiet and open countryside of the northern edge of the North Pennines Area of Outstanding Natural Beauty is only revealed as a centre of former industrial activity to those who bother to take a closer look on foot. There are some fine views from the walk route. In several places the ground is marshy and you should be prepared to jump some ditches and streams.

The Walk

Stand and look across from the pub door for a moment before you move off. Over the road, at right angles, is the former Naworth Collieries Co-operative Society Ltd, which still continues as a shop despite the demise of the former industrial life of the area. Turn to the right and walk along the Clowsgill lane. The buildings are all made of yellow-grey Pennine sandstone. This springs into life with a warm glow in sunshine but glowers flatly under a dull sky. The Wesleyan chapel (1883), on the left, has red sandstone decoration from the valley 500 ft below. Go right up the farm track on the path for Highfell. To your left the great sweep of the northern end of the North Pennines dips down towards the Tyne valley; the area is usually referred to as the Tindale Fells, the northernmost summit being Cold Fell at 2,041 feet.

Walk round the bend and straight between the house and barns of Clement Leazes, then ahead into the field. Swing to the left along the boundary by an old belt of beech trees. Bear half-right now on the path between the wooden gateposts and cross the field to a stone stile onto a lane. Turn left up the lane and pass the buildings of Highfell Farm and its copse of trees to the right. At the far end, turn left between the old and the new buildings on the bridleway for Park Terrace. As you cross the field the view around is very wide – the Solway Firth catches the sun to the far left, Kershope Forest should be visible up by the Scottish border, and the village lies below with the modern quarry of Silvertop across the main

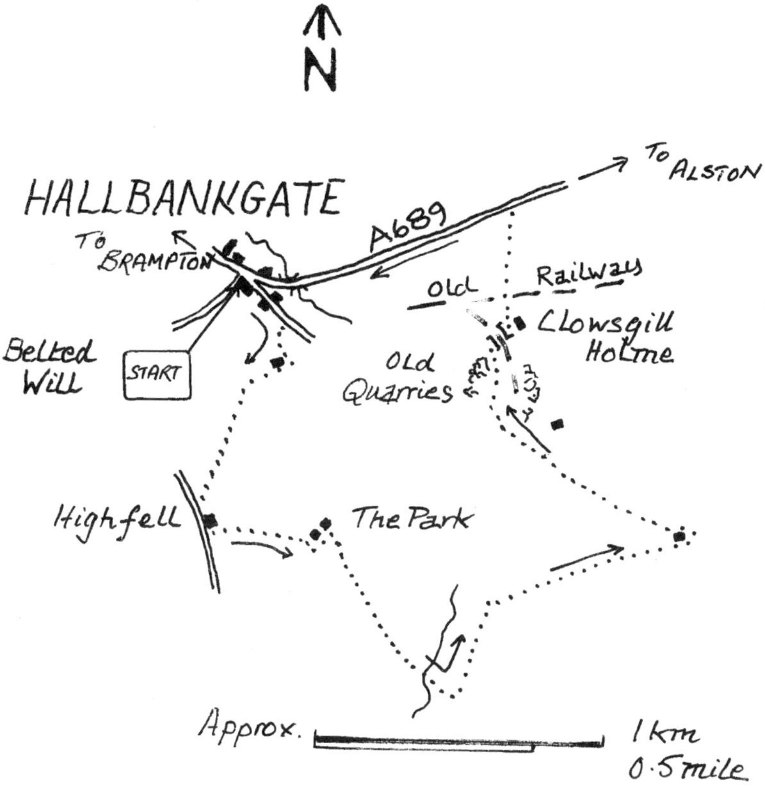

road to its right. Cross the field on the track and turn left to go in front of the hamlet of houses at The Park – a university research station is based here. Take the stile to the right.

Mount the brow at right angles and look for the faint line of an old track heading for the white cottage of Tortie, which you can see on the far side of the shallow valley. To the right of the cottage is a bank of former limekilns. Cross a marshy section of the field to a stone stile to the left of a wall gap and bear right a little to go round a marshy area and jump a ditch. Fine sunny days find the air here filled with the cry of curlew and the song of the skylark. Look for a gateway with a limestone post in the wall ahead and find a stone stile in the wall between this and the wire fence which lies at right angles on the far side. Cross over and go down to negotiate the Cleskett beck by using one of the larger stones in the water. Rise to the field gate and exit onto a track. Go left for 250 yards to the end of the metalled road.

Take the track labelled for Tarn House (ignore the 'No Road' sign –

which applies to vehicles) and rise gently round the shoulder of Tortie Hill. At the little enclosure of Thorn, on your left, admire the view down Tindale to the tarn, now a reserve, and across to Stagsike, in the trees.

The route of the bridleway goes all the way round the back of the walled enclosure and through the gate on the far side from the track (off which there is no sign). Aim towards the houses of Park Terrace and cross over the marshy and rush-filled field to descend slowly to a gate about 100 yards to the left of a cottage which stands on the edge of the old Clowsgill quarries. Follow the track through the hummocks and across. The remains of limekilns, the former waterwheel pit and inclines are still visible. Go over the obvious bed of a railway track and turn right opposite an isolated white cottage called Closegill. Drop down and pass under the bridge to go in front of Clowsgill Holme. In a field close by, not a lifetime ago, hundreds gathered for the Methodist Camp Meeting every Whitsuntide.

Keep ahead through the dismantled railway bridge. The railway remains relate to both the quarries and the extensive coal mines, developed by the Earl of Carlisle, which existed around Tindale and Midgeholme (which gives its name to this outlying coalfield) and for which Hallbankgate was the centre until the 1950s. Stephenson's famous 'Rocket' ended its working days here before it reached the Science Museum in London. At Kirkhouse, on the Brampton side of the village, there were even a gasworks, coke ovens and foundries capable of building locomotives on occasion.

Walk through to the main road. Turn left along the verge, with some care for traffic, and re-enter the village past the entrance to Silvertop quarry. Opposite the garage is a large pheasantry and, as you cross the little beck, a small green which has been lovingly cared for. The pub stands at the top of the brow.

27 Nenthead
The Miners Arms

Nenthead is a planned early 19th-century creation (started about 1825) by the London Lead Company which had, by then, become the successor to a long line of mining enterprises in the area. The search for lead and, equally importantly, the silver which accompanied it, may well have begun with the Romans. Zinc has been mined too. At over 1,400 ft, and with the top of the road at more than 2,000 ft, Nenthead claims to be the highest village, have the highest church, the highest vicarage, the highest Methodist chapel, the highest village hall and, even, the highest house in England (strangely, no one seems to claim the accolade of the highest pub for the Miners Arms). The character of the Pennine sandstone of which the inn is built gives it a tough and uncompromising face which the present owners have successfully softened, both outside and in.

Food is available from 12 noon to 2 pm and from 7 pm to 8.45 pm each day; breakfast, tea and coffee are also served. The first Tuesday in each month is a speciality night and it is no surprise that awards such as 'Pub Dish of the Year', for the Alston pie, and 'Bar Snack of Great Britain', for the leek and Stilton pot, have been won. The menu is extensive and wide ranging, with no less than eight vegetarian offerings as standard. Snack meals are out of the ordinary too, for example the jacket potatoes here are filled with the local Alston cheese. No one, including the children, should feel themselves other than spoiled for choice!

John Smith's ales are the standard draught at this freehouse, but they are accompanied by three guest beers each week, so the annual selection is considerable. Stout is Guinness, the lager Carlsberg export and the cider Strongbow. Opening times are 11 am to 11 pm on Mondays to Saturdays, 12 noon to 3 pm and 7 pm to 10.30 on Sundays. There is a small outside terrace above the road. Dogs are most welcome. A public children's play area is located immediately across the road. The Miners Arms also offers accommodation.

Telephone: 01434 381427.

How to get there: The pub stands beside the village crossroads on the A689, between Alston and Weardale.

Parking: Outside the pub or across the road by the Visitor Centre access.

Length of the walk: 3½ miles. Map: OS Landranger 86 Haltwhistle, Bewcastle and Alston (pub GR 781437).

The valley of the river Nent was, not so long ago, the centre of extensive mining operations. The remains form one of the richest sites of our industrial heritage. The valley has slowly returned to rural peacefulness and is particularly attractive for its wildflowers in summer. The walk route climbs high up the valley side.

The Walk

Go left from the pub door and walk to the far side of the crossroads. In the angle of the roads, to the left, is what was probably the first ever purpose-built library building in the country – London Lead, as a Quaker company, believed strongly that a well-educated workforce was a better one (the building now houses the over 60s club). It is even recorded that 'the miners prefer books to drink'. Across the lane is the fine public fountain (1877) with dome and decorated cast iron. Cross over the main road and continue towards the bridge as far as the entrance to the Rampgill Mine Visitor Centre car park, walking up to the buildings of the centre. This is a development by the North Pennines Heritage Trust and includes a museum of the mining industry as well as modern craft workshops.

A lengthy visit is well worthwhile and you may wish to inspect the massive mine site in detail – there are over 300 acres in all. (Notices of the danger of the old shafts and unstable buildings are posted and care should be taken, especially if children are in the party.) In any case, it is worth

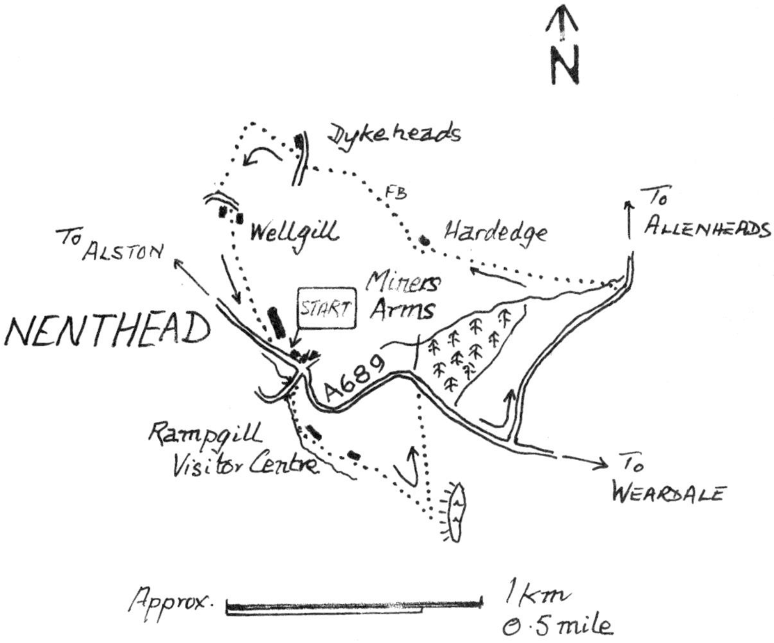

walking through the site, past the mine manager's house on the brow to the left, and going along the upper track as far as the embankment of the small contour reservoir. The view of the whole site, including the smelter, from the top of this is very good indeed.

Retrace your steps from here to the gate onto the path which runs due north, on the east side of the Gillgill burn opposite the house. Wind your way among the old spoil heaps and water channels and bear left by the upright stone with the arrow, following the rough track across the burn to reach a gate onto the A689 by some white cottages. In summer, along the way, you will find masses of wild pansies – heartsease – purple, yellow, and both together; curlews and oystercatchers fly overhead and, maybe, the occasional peregrine too. Turn up the verge to the right, past a struggling plantation of Scots pine and larch and an old milestone. On the left is a dramatic exposure of the layers of sandstone and shale rocks in the small gill. Continue as far as the left turn for Coalcleugh and Allenheads, marked 'B6293'.

Tall black and white posts line the roadside to indicate it during the inevitable snow, which drifts even in mild winters. The road climbs gently and you can see the plantation to the left around the Gillgill burn more clearly. The trees have often died, or barely struggle on, because of the lead which poisons the earth. In amongst these old spoil heaps a very specialist assemblage of plants survives the pollution. Some 100 yards after the road crosses the burn a path goes off left for High House. Go over the boggy patch to a stone stile in the wall and bear left a little before going fractionally right to a yellow-topped post marking a stile in the far wall. You may need to divert a little round the peaty area and then the line of the path becomes more obvious along the left-hand wall to the farm ruin. The view across the valley is spectacular – the upper part of the Rampgill site is in view and the road climbs from the village steeply up towards Garrigill; half-right are the Tindale Fells and the Tyne Gap. Pass above the buildings and to two stiles over a track on a path for Dykeheads. Drop down to the footbridge over the burn and go left to the yellow-topped post. Away from the mine pollution the summer flowers are lush – lady's mantles, mayflowers, globeflowers and kingcups. Cross two fields (the second is very wet) to a track and turn down to the left to the lane.

The route goes right now for Pry House, and then left through the yard. Use the stile to the left of the building and follow the yellow arrow through the gate, dropping diagonally to the bottom right-hand corner of the field. Do not use the obvious stile, but turn left on the clear green track and cross the field back towards the village. Follow the markers past the house and drop to meet the lane. Go left over the gill and immediately bear right between the houses at Wellgill. Take the path for Nenthead and angle down above the sewage works on the marked path to reach the river Nent across from the reclaimed site of the former mine washing area. The church of St John (1845), with its polygonal turret for the bells, lies up to the left; some of the inside fittings certainly came from much older buildings. Pass Hilverston Terrace, stone houses, and exit to the road close to the bus garage of Wright Brothers. This occupies a building put up by the German firm of Krupp when the Belgian Vielle Montagne Company took over the mines in 1886, and housed the plant for concentrating the ore. Its industrial archaeological value outweighs by far its attractiveness. Walk back to the pub in 50 yards.

It is but a mile or two to Alston, England's highest market town. Its covered market cross is a fine one and High Mill waterwheel is virtually in the town centre. Steam trains of the South Tynedale Railway run from Alston station throughout most of the year (telephone: 01434 381696). Over the hill eastwards, in County Durham, is the lead mine and massive waterwheel at Killhope. Over the hill, northwards, is the Heritage Centre of Allenheads in Northumberland. All are worth linking with this walk.

28 Garrigill
The George and Dragon Inn

Garrigill is a remote spot and is the furthest village in the upper valley of the river South Tyne, which drains this eastern section of Cumbria to the North Sea, rather than to the Irish Sea. Unusually, the village name seems to be a Norman French one, and simply means 'Gerard's valley' – who Gerard was and why he managed to impart his name to an area still scattered with many much older ones is lost in the mists of both time and of the North Pennines. Once upon a time, a road ran over the fell to the Eden valley and the George and Dragon was a coaching inn which, in the 17th century (it was built about 1621), served its users. It forms part of a terraced frontage which opens directly to the street and its plain sandstone exterior catches the warming sun only early in the day. Inside, the open fireplace in the bar and the low ceiling take you back in time, ensuring a warm welcome at all times of the day and in all seasons. Overnight accommodation is still available here.

Food is served daily from 12 noon to 2 pm and 7 pm to 9 pm. Traditional staples, like steak pie and gammon rashers, remain very much in demand and have been joined, these days, by popular vegetarian choices. Snacks of sandwiches and filled jacket potatoes are varied and the children have their own menu to choose from.

This is a freehouse and stocks a range of Theakston (BB and XB) and Scottish and Newcastle (Exhibition, McEwan 70/-, Best Scotch) beers. The stout is Gillespies, the lager McEwan's and the cider is Strongbow. House wine is available. Outside food service hours you are welcome to bring your own picnic. Dogs are not permitted inside the inn.

Telephone: 01434 381293.

How to get there: The road beyond the village is a dead-end for cars. Approach along narrow lanes (some with steep hills), following signs off the B6277, the Alston to Middleton in Teesdale road, or the A686, the Alston to Penrith road.

Parking: There is no car park at the pub but plenty of roadside parking is available in the village.

Length of the walk: 2½ miles. Map: OS Landranger 86 Haltwhistle, Bewcastle and Alston (inn GR 745415).

Part of the North Pennines Area of Outstanding Natural Beauty, this is remote country and prone to mists and winter snows. In summer, however, it is fine, flowery countryside with wide views and the gorge of the South Tyne and the Ashgill waterfalls are most attractive. The lead mining past is almost all gone here. The climb out of Ash Gill is stepped at the steepest part and the rest is easy going.

The Walk

Take a short tour round the village green, with its shady lime trees, before you set off. This is another of those Pennine villages which grew out of lead and zinc mining. Mine owners were surprisingly forward-looking and built housing for their employees which would last. Even in lead mining days the employees themselves lasted well too. John Martin and his wife sat down to a celebration tea on this green at the passing of the Reform Bill of 1832 – they were both 102 years of age! The old school is pre-1865 and shows the interesting regional feature of this part of the country in its white, decorative stone courses. Walk off the green southwards, in the direction of Moorhouse. Just along to the left is the church of St John the Evangelist. Probably, like me, you will have to untie the gate because the graveyard is usually full of grazing sheep – much cheaper and more effective, I'm sure, than lawnmowers. Originally a chapelry of Alston, it dates from before 1215 but was much altered in Victorian times. There are some gloriously decorated organ pipes and a medieval water stoup.

Return to the road and go left to pass a house which has had a modern oriel window added to it. Walk on to Gatehead where there is a fine

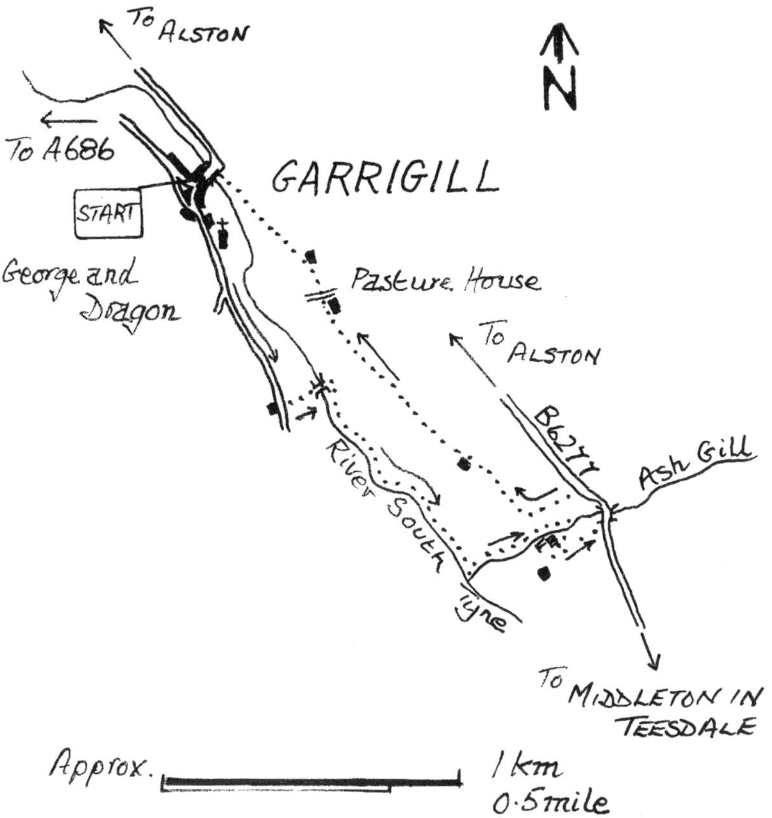

Primitive Methodist chapel of 1885. The road you have been on, and that to the right, are part of the Pennine Way (which runs from the Peak District to the Scots border). Along to the right, too, is the Moor House National Nature Reserve, a World Biosphere Reserve for its unique peaty blanket, its plants and birds. This is the old corpse road by which bodies were transported for burial at Kirkland round the shoulder of Cross Fell. It may explain why this part of the country is in Cumbria at all instead of being part of Northumberland. Press straight on, however, up the brow. Beside the road, near the old hand-pump, grow unusually large and lush knapweeds with wine-red flower heads. At the next farm on the right, Low Crossgill, turn left down the track, passing a hogg hole with its closing stone in place (a sheep gap in the wall), and drop to the oddly curved Windshaw Bridge. Downstream from the bridge is a fine gorge with a profusion of mosses and ferns growing in the damp shade.

Walk right along the east bank of the river and cross a series of stone stiles. Many of the fields are small and narrow, for it was common for miners' families to be smallholders as well and for the women, especially, to try to keep them self-sufficient in food. The bank is lined with ash, birch, alder, rowan, sycamore and elm and the river bed becomes gorge-like again. On occasion you may come across parties of youngsters being led up river, through the water, as they get a taste of what it is like really to combat the forces of nature. Eventually, you will reach Ash Gill, coming in from the left, and will have to go up to the footbridge by the fence. Go ahead through the kissing gate and up to the waterfalls. The lower fall tumbles over flat, horizontal beds of rock, but the upper cascades in one dramatic drop; reach it over the higher footbridge. It isn't, in fact, all that high but the road bridge above it makes it look bigger and it gives the rare opportunity – if you don't mind the chance of getting a bit wet – of actually walking behind the fall. Exit from the gorge up the cliff, on the south side, by the angled permissive path amongst orchids, water dropwort and ferns. As the path bends back up the gill near the top there are deep eroded fissures in the limestone. A set of steps leads up to the road south of the sandstone bridge.

Cross over the bridge and turn left on the footpath in 50 yards. Do not follow straight down, but bear half-right, through the broken wall and across the field towards the buildings of Ashgillside (1734). The view across the valley is excellent and takes in both Moor House and Cross Fell on a fine day. Use the stone stile at the top side of the buildings and follow the arrows through the far buildings, with their typical stone-flagged roofs, to a stone stile to the right by a new barn. The path contours along the hillside and crosses a stone stile to run below Pasture House. Beyond the village, down the valley, you will be able to see the mix of woodland and pasture so familiar in the North Pennine valleys. Here and there are shake holes, where cave roofs have collapsed, and scatterings of old mine workings. Cross over the metalled lane and walk along the track to bear left between the buildings, then drop half-right across the field to a stile in the bottom corner. Stone steps lead to a built-up path and you angle gently down to the village at the bridge. Pass over this and along by the public toilets to return to the inn.

29 Kirkoswald
The Crown Inn

The tiny former market town of Kirkoswald, much of it built out of red sandstone blocks robbed from the castle, was preserved by the happy chance of the railway line passing down the Eden valley on the far bank of the river in the 1870s. Three pubs still stand beside the cobbled market place, of which one is the Crown. The newest building on the square is the village institute of 1910 and the cottage right next to the pub bears the date 1757 – and my guess is that the Crown is of roughly the same age. It was once, certainly, a market pub and its low-beamed interior speaks strongly of yesteryear.

All food is freshly prepared on the spot and a speciality is made of fresh fish, bought off the quay at North Shields, on the Tyne. Clearly, only the specials board for the day can announce the current delectation. The more standard menu gives a wide choice, in any case, and Sunday roasts and a selection of curries are very popular. A variety of snacks and sandwiches are available and children's portions are served. An unusual offering is a take-out service, much used by those using local self-catering accommodation. Serving times are 11 am (noon on Sundays) to 2.30 pm and 6 pm (6.30 pm on Sundays) to about 10 pm.

This is part of the Pubmaster group of inns and so carries a selection of beers from several breweries. At the time of writing, these were Worthingon BB, Newcastle Exhibition, and Mitchells and Butlers Mild. Tennents lager, Guinness and Dry Blackthorn cider complete the range. Bar hours are 11 am to 3.30 pm (4 pm on Saturdays), and 12 noon to 3.30 pm on Sundays; in the evening it opens at 5.30 pm (6.30 pm on Sundays) until 11 pm (10.30 pm on Sundays).

Telephone: 01768 898435.

How to get there: The pub is beside the B6413 in the centre of the village. The shortest approach is from the A6 at Plumpton, north of Penrith, and then via Lazonby. From the north, approach via Brampton or the A6 and Armathwaite.

Parking: The pub has a couple of spaces only. There is public parking on the market square immediately adjacent.

Length of the walk: 5¼ miles. Extensions to the church and castle would add half a mile. Map: OS Landranger 86 Haltwhistle, Bewcastle and Alston (inn GR 555401).

Three contrasting aspects make up this walk. The little town itself deserves some time and can be taken either first or last. The valley of the Raven beck is quiet and partly wooded, with a variety of birdlife. The circuit back, via Scales Hall, takes you up, fairly gently, onto the wind-blown lower slopes of the North Pennines.

The Walk

Turn right from the pub door and take the first left beside Bank House. Pass the doctors' surgery on your right and walk ahead beside the, now dry, mill leet on your left. In a few yards this crosses the track and a junction in it feeds a metal trough across the beck to the sawmill on the far side. The beck rushes between steep, rocky banks in a mini-gorge from the mill weir by the field gate. Cross the field on a clear path and enter the wood through a kissing-gate, then bear right for Parkhead at the fingerpost. A short, muddy stretch through willows leads on to a section where tall spruces tower up amongst the broadleaved trees. A footbridge across the beck to the right should be ignored (as should a further three you will pass). Move out into open fields again and follow the right-hand boundary alongside mixed woodland which stands on the winter flood debris of the beck. There are glimpses up the valley to the skyline of the Pennines ahead and a few areas of arable can be picked out here and there. Buzzards wheel over the plantations, grey wagtails skip over the stones of the beck and mixed flocks of tits search for insects on the bark of the trees in autumn and winter. The whole area is alive with pheasants in autumn.

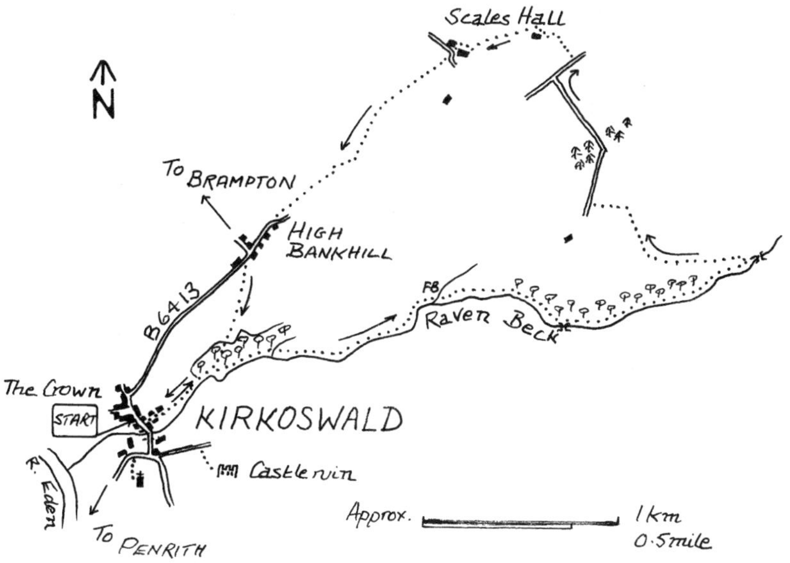

Eventually you reach a footbridge across the Nether Haresceugh Gill, just beside a steel farm bridge. Cross over and use the stile, continuing up river through the next field and entering woodland again. There is a clear track through a plantation of poplars and the valley narrows, the sides almost becoming cliffs in places. At a farm bridge, stay on the same side of the beck along the narrowing path and pass a small brick shed, on the far bank, which houses a steadily chugging water ram-pump. Pass an old quarry on the left and walk along a section of path which has been cut into the bank above the water. Beyond the stone stile in the wall the grazed left-hand bank is covered in large oak trees and you will come to an obvious rock overhang at the base of a small cliff.

Before reaching the stile and bridge over the beck, take the green track left on the nearside of the wall and bear back up the slope of the field. Pass through the steel gate, then walk along the right-hand boundary and through a second gate. Continue beside the right-hand boundary wall and bend round to the right to a third gate. Go straight ahead to the far side of the field. Join the green track along the wall to the left to reach a metalled lane with farm buildings down on your left. The view has opened up as you have climbed the brow – behind is Hartside and the summit of Cross Fell, in front is the distinctive saddle-shaped outline of Blencathra amongst the northern Lakeland fells.

Turn right up the lane beside a new plantation, cross through a belt of

Scots pines and walk up to the junction. Go right for 100 yards and turn left on the track towards Scale Rigg. Your path goes to the right through the gate beside the near end of the barn and passes the rear of the house to the left-hand of a pair of gates. Aim across the next two fields for the buildings of Scales Hall. The view to the left of the Pennine escarpment now includes the two detached hills of Knock and Dufton Pikes. A stile leads to the track at the nearside of the barns and you need to walk to the right through the farmyard and out to the lane. Go 5 yards to the left and find the stone stile on the right into the field. Cross over to a stile in the corner by the gate and keep the same line to a second stile in the far fence (both these were in poor condition when I last walked through). Walk up the slope to the right-hand of a pair of gates ahead and follow through along the left-hand boundary row of trees as far as the corner of the fence. Turn hard right and cross the field to the junction of the hedge line (many are crab apples) and fence, then bear left to a short section of wall in which there is a stile. Continue straight ahead to the bottom left-hand corner of the field and a further stone stile onto a lane. Turn right and walk to the corner of the B6413 at High Bankhill. A few yards to the right is a rare example of a cottage with a thatched roof.

Go straight ahead, past the parish notice board and find the iron kissing-gate to the left opposite the houses. Bear diagonally right across the field to a stile in the wall and cross the next, much larger, field to a stile into the wood at its bottom corner. Drop sharply down the bank to the right and follow the clear path amongst the trees to reach the fingerpost again. Turn back right to return to the village street.

In the village, walk around the market place. The war memorial cross stands where the old stocks used to be and outside the Bull Inn the ring in the pavement marks where baiting took place. Beyond Bank House, on the left is a fine Queen Anne house dated 1703 and a cottage of 1713. Many of the other buildings are most attractive too. Cross over the bridge. Round to the left, and a short way along a footpath, are the ruins of the castle – mostly a moat, bank, and much of one tower. The other tower on the hillock across the way is the only example of a detached bell tower, or campanile, in the county. The present one is a rebuilding of 1893. The actual entrance to the church is a few yards down the Penrith road along a paved path amongst lime trees. Around the year AD 640 King Oswald of Northumbria was here with St Aidan and the holy well which issues from beneath the west end of the church is dedicated to Oswald. The building has been much altered over the centuries but has plenty of interest within. Lord Dacre founded a college of priests here as late as 1523 and the fine building, which you can make out through the archway across the road from the church path, is known as the College, home of the Fethersonhaughs for four centuries. Most of what you see is of 1696, but older parts are based round a defensive pele tower.

30 Langwathby
The Shepherds Inn

The 'village by the long ford' remains a major crossing point of the river Eden. The ford was replaced by a stone bridge in 1685 but this collapsed in the floods of March 1968 and was replaced by the one-track, steel-girder structure which has now become the image which stays in the mind for the many users of the main road through the valley. Stopping at the Shepherds Inn, which has stood on the green since the 1700s, should readily restore the balance. Although refurbished, it retains some of its original wooden beams and an open fireplace in the lounge. Standing at the doorway and looking north along the green puts a quite different perspective on the village.

Food is available here from 12 noon to 2 pm and 6.30 pm to 8.30 pm each day. The lunchtime menu includes the snacks for the passing trade and some items are not served in the evening. A surprise main course, halfway across England from sea to sea, is battered squid, but you might follow that with a more country-style pudding of blackberry and apple pancakes. Children's portions are served and there are vegetarian choices.

This is a Whitbread pub and has Trophy ale and Dark Mild on draught. These are supplemented by Castle Eden and Boddingtons beers. The stout is Guinness, the lager Heineken and the cider is Bulmer's Original. The bar opens from 11 am to 3 pm and 6.30 pm to 11 pm (10.30 pm on Sundays). Families are welcome and there is a pleasant beer garden.

Telephone: 01768 881335.

How to get there: The Shepherds stands on the green in the centre of the village beside the A686, between Penrith and Alston. The village is served by the Settle to Carlisle railway line (the station is only a quarter of a mile from the inn).

Parking: At the inn.

Length of the walk: 3¼ miles. Maps: OS Landranger 90 Penrith, Keswick and Ambleside and 91 Appleby (inn GR 569335).

Langwathby itself is typical of Danish green-village settlements of the Eden valley. The walk, easy going underfoot, passes beside the river Eden, with a wealth of wildlife to be seen. The church of St Cuthbert, at Edenhall, is outstanding and the village has some gems of its own.

The Walk

It is well worth starting by walking around the village green. As with other villages in this area in the past, Langwathby green was surrounded by small farmhouses with attached smallholdings of 25 to 30 acres. These days, the red sandstone houses are dwellings – often for commuters to Carlisle – and the farms have amalgamated into larger holdings, so it remains a working agricultural community. On the east side is the small church of St Peter. Rebuilt in 1718, with Victorian additions, it contains traces of its earlier ancestry and some 17th-century armour.

Exit from the green in the direction of Penrith and walk along the footway in front of a row of sandstone cottages and then down the grass verge to the bridge. A footwalk crosses on the downstream side. On the far bank, cross over the main road and go along the path beside the river, marked for Edenhall. On this bank the land is flat and set with crops of winter wheat. These flat 'halks' flood in winter, so revitalising the soil. The steep east bank, below the village, is dotted with cherry trees whose blossom stands out in spring. At the same time of year the alder and willow along the bank are interspersed with daffodils and butterbur as well as the flood litter of the winter. On the river you can often see swans, mallards, tufted ducks, mergansers, oystercatchers and common sandpipers. Rooks nest in the pines. At the gate by the wood divert up a little, to avoid the landslip, and walk along a row of beech. The view is fine – to the east lie Cross Fell, Great Dun Fell and Dufton Pike, up the valley is Nine Standards Rigg, by Kirkby Stephen. Under the coppice hazel in spring, at the far end of the bank, are celandines and drifts of snowdrops

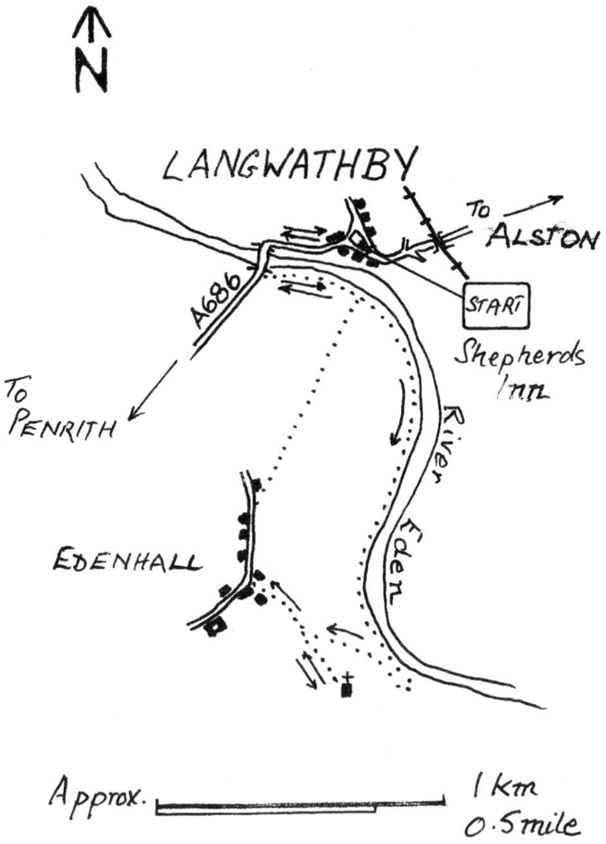

with anemones scattered here and there. Go down the steps to join the built up 'Ladies' Walk' with polypody ferns growing out of the upper wall. Stay up and go through the gate at the far end, then bear hard right, up the bank, to walk across the field on a track to the gate.

The cross, at the junction of tracks, marks the spot where, in 1870, a water trough was removed. This may have served the village of Edenhall in plague times as a stone on which money could be left for the payment for goods. Go left to the church of St Cuthbert. Traditionally, this is one of the many churches which marks the resting place of the body of St Cuthbert during the seven-year wanderings of his monks after the Danish invasion of Lindisfarne in AD 875 – certainly a small, blocked-up window on the north wall of the nave could be of Saxon age. At one time the manor was in the hands of the Bruces (of whom Robert the Bruce remains the most famous) but came, in 1327, to the Stapletons and then, in 1468, to the

Musgraves. A monumental brass in the chancel to Sir William Stapleton and his wife is one of the finest in England (now carefully preserved from vandalism). One of the bells dates from around 1400 and the windows are interesting, too, and make for a light and airy interior. Perhaps the most famous item of all (now in the Victoria and Albert Museum in London) is the 'Luck of Edenhall', a 14th-century Venetian glass beaker – perhaps brought back by a crusader – in an embossed leather case, of which there are several representations. Superstition has it that while the 'Luck' is preserved so will the fortunes of the Musgraves prosper. Quite how this fits in with the demolition of the former classical mansion of Edenhall (1821–1934) is difficult to see!

'If e'er this cup shall break or fall
Farewell the luck of Eden Hall'

Longfellow wrote a poem about the 'Luck' (based on one by a German, J. L. Uhland) after having been entertained at the hall and having actually been pressed to drink from the glass itself.

Return past the cross and exit to the village past the east lodge, Tea Rose House and Corner Cottage – quite clearly buildings of considerable age. Divert to the left for 50 yards to look at the former stable block and coach house of the demolished hall. A fine clock tower remains and keeps accurate time. Across the road are estate cottages of 1877 (the Musgrave coat of arms on all the estate buildings is always obvious). Walk back, past the war memorial, cottages with stone slab roofs and the Edenhall Hotel to Rosewall Cottage (1847) with its odd blank oriel-cum-dormer above the porch. Take the path beside it and go down the brow, beside the shelterbelt of pines, towards the river. Back, over your shoulder, you can see the plantations on the ridge behind Penrith town and ahead is the massive scarp slope of the North Pennines. Turn left at the river bank and retrace your steps over the bridge to reach the village and the start once more. The river has inspired several writers: Wordsworth, of course, John Stagg, 'the blind bard of Cumberland' (1770–1823), who collected folktales and folksongs of the county, and Drayton, who wrote of it in his *Polyolbion* of 1622.

Two other interesting places are very close by and you might well combine this walk with visits to them. Barely a mile and a half north is Little Salkeld Mill (open on weekdays throughout the year). This is a water-powered 17th-century mill which produces organic flours. About 4 miles south, and actually on the former Westmorland side of the Crowdundle beck, is the National Trust property of Acorn Bank. This is famous for its varieties of daffodil and narcissus, amongst many other wild and cultivated plants, and has the most famous herb garden in the North. Opening is from April to the end of October.